# YUMMY LITTLE BELLY

**WHEN USING KITCHEN APPLIANCES PLEASE ALWAYS FOLLOW THE MANUFACTURER'S INSTRUCTIONS**

HarperCollins*Publishers*
1 London Bridge Street
London SE1 9GF

www.harpercollins.co.uk

HarperCollins*Publishers*
Macken House
39/40 Mayor Street Upper
Dublin 1, D01 C9W8, Ireland

First published by
HarperCollins*Publishers* 2024

2 3 4 5 6 7 8 9

© Romina Bertinazzo 2024
Paediatric dietician: Lucy Upton
Photography © Andrew Burton

Romina Bertinazzo asserts the moral right
to be identified as the author of this work

A catalogue record of this book is
available from the British Library

ISBN 978-0-00-870016-4

Photographer: Andrew Burton
Food Stylist: Rosie Reynolds
Prop Stylist: Charlie Phillips

Printed and bound by GPS Group, Bosnia-Herzegovina

This book contains FSC™ certified paper and other controlled
sources to ensure responsible forest management.

For more information visit: www.harpercollins.co.uk/green

Romina Bertinazzo

# YUMMY LITTLE BELLY

**Over 80 quick, easy
nutritious recipes to keep you
and your little ones happy!**

Thorsons

# DEDICATION

To my husband Mattia, my daughters Grace and Kate,
and my followers: thank you for your unwavering support
and love. This book is dedicated to you.

# CONTENTS

# FOREWORD

As a children's dietitian and nutritionist, I understand the critical role nutrition plays in the early years of a child's life. It's widely recognised that these formative years are crucial for establishing the groundwork for their later health, and, as parents, nutrition is one of the factors we have the power to influence, amidst many others beyond our control. Despite this, parents are expected to cut through the (increasingly loud) noise when it comes to nutrition and feeding advice for their babies and children.

In my work, I help to translate the complex world of nutrition science into digestible and research-backed information that you can understand. I'm constantly seeking resources that guide parents in serving up this knowledge to children and in answering the question: what do we actually put on our children's plates?

Positive feeding foundations for children also include how they are fed. If you were to ask me to choose one priority when it comes to how to feed your children, I'd tell you to prioritise doing it as a family. There is a saying in Italian, 'La famiglia è tutto', which translates to 'family is everything'. It is a saying that I couldn't resonate more with when it comes to mealtimes. The evidence behind the benefits of eating as a family is longstanding and convincing, extending far beyond supporting children to eat a balanced and varied diet. So, when I was asked to review this book, you can imagine my delight in seeing recipes that were not only colourful, varied and nutritionally balanced, but that were evidently written with eating together in mind.

Romina has managed to inspire an avid audience of parents with her simple, nutritious meals that are easy to make but also bring mealtimes back to family, connection, exploration and fun! Romina's infectious enthusiasm for food, her culture and her family are celebrated throughout this book, which is packed full of delicious and creative recipes that will tantalise your little ones' taste buds and get you thinking about feeding children in a whole new way. With each page turned, you'll discover not just a collection of dishes, but a roadmap to joyful and wholesome family meals. You'll also have peace of mind that there is always an answer to 'What shall I prepare for dinner tonight?' just an arm's reach away.

I trust you'll enjoy this remarkable book as much as I have cherished being a small part of its creation.

## Lucy Upton
Specialist Paediatric Dietitian

# INTRODUCTION

As I write this, I'm sitting on the train heading to the first day of the photoshoot for my book – the very one you're holding! I'm trying to pen an introduction to one of the most exciting chapters of my career. Who would have thought four years ago that I, the ultimate digital antisocial, would be running an Instagram page with over a million followers and be on the verge of becoming a cookbook author?

For those who don't already know me, I want to share a bit about my story and how Yummy Little Belly came into being. I was born and raised in a small town in northern Italy. You wouldn't guess it from the recipes I share now, but as a child, I categorically refused to eat any fruit or vegetables and only loved chocolate; I was a true fussy eater!

As I grew up, I developed an interest in healthy eating and cooking. Ever since I was a teenager, I loved experimenting with new recipes. At the age of 22, following a romantic breakup, I decided to escape. My friend Mattia helped me move to London to work as an au pair. After a few weeks, Mattia and I unexpectedly fell in love, and he is now my husband. Admittedly, life in London was a real challenge: finding yourself in a country where you don't speak the language, without friends or family and having to rely only on your own strength is an experience that really made me grow up and mature as a person.

For the first few years, we lived in Paddington in a very small room in a shared house; it was a great experience, but after a while, we felt the need to have a place of our own and moved to an apartment outside London. In 2019, we had our first daughter, Grace.

When it became time for weaning, I had no idea what to prepare for her. I wanted to give her nutritious and simple meals that were also appealing for all the family. I was firmly convinced of two things: I did not want to give Grace shop-bought or processed food but rather feed her healthy dishes made with ingredients I knew, and I wanted to maintain the habit of eating together as a family.

I believe this tradition of eating together was fundamental in weaning Grace and later Kate, my younger daughter, and an integral part of their food education. Often, when I share photos of our family dinners on social media, I am asked why the girls eat so late or why Mattia and I don't carve out time for ourselves by having the girls eat earlier. Honestly, this made me think a lot, as this isn't something Mattia and I imposed, but a natural choice, probably cultural, based on how we grew up in Italy.

Dissatisfied with the vague information I found online, often not aligned with my Mediterranean cuisine, I decided to start sharing our everyday dishes on Instagram. I launched the Yummy Little Belly page on a Saturday afternoon in March 2020, just for fun. The first post I shared was my recipe for banana and blueberry pancakes. I aimed to offer simple recipes to help other parents who found themselves in the same situation I was in. I began to share the dishes I prepared daily for Grace: quick dishes that did not require much time to prepare but were above all healthy and of which I was proud.

The Covid-19 lockdown arrived and Yummy Little Belly became my refuge during those months when we were all staying at home. I started receiving daily messages of thanks from other parents, who told me how useful my page was for them, sending me photos of their children eating my recipes. It was the best feeling!

Instagram was a revelation; I never imagined I could create such a united and supportive community. Initially, I thought I was doing something good for other parents, but I quickly realised that as the community grew, they were a huge support for me in many difficult situations and made me feel less alone in this chaotic and wonderful journey that is motherhood.

I hope the recipes in my book can inspire you and help you in the wonderful adventure of weaning! I cannot wait to see all your creations – buon appetito!

## A NOTE ON INGREDIENTS

Added salt and sugar (including alternatives such as maple syrup) should be avoided for babies under 1 year old, so the recipes in this book are written to reflect that. See page 13 for more guidance on foods to limit for babies.

## CHEESE

Recipes that included Parmesan and other cheeses have been listed as vegetarian, but please check the ingredients and ensure specific products are suitable for you if you follow a vegetarian diet, or else choose a similar vegetarian alternative. Though Parmesan has a relatively high salt content, the amounts used in the recipes are suitable for babies.

Mozzarella features in a few recipes throughout this book, so it's worth bearing in mind that although it is softer than a lot of other cheeses you might give to a baby or child, and therefore easier to swallow, it still presents a choking risk. To reduce this risk, avoid offering cheese in cubes or small balls, or as lumps of melted cheese. Instead, always cut mozzarella into thin slices.

# WEANING: THE BIG QUESTIONS

Starting solids is a thrilling yet challenging phase for us parents, right? With an abundance of information online, it can feel like diving into a sea of uncertainty. But fear not! I've teamed up with Lucy, an experienced children's dietitian and nutritionist, to make this journey smoother. Together, we've curated a comprehensive Q&A to address everyday worries and concerns. I have posed all the big questions, and Lucy has provided her expert response. From selecting those crucial first foods to managing potential allergies and ensuring a balanced diet, we've got you covered. Let's navigate this exciting milestone with confidence!

**Q. HOW CAN I TELL WHEN MY BABY IS READY TO START SOLIDS?**

**A.** Current guidance in the UK is that babies should start solids at around 6 months old, and not before 4 months. I encourage parents to focus on their baby and look for the developmental signs that their baby is ready to start learning to eat, such as:

- Your baby can sit for a short time unsupported.
- Your baby can hold their head upright.
- Your baby can coordinate picking something up and bringing it to their mouth.
- Your baby's tongue thrust reflex starts to diminish; for example, they can keep food in their mouth, not just push it out!

**Q. WHAT ARE THE BEST FOODS TO START WEANING WITH?**

**A.** There is no correct answer here. Some research suggests that starting with single tastes of bitter vegetables such as spinach, courgette and broccoli can help a baby continue to accept these foods later into weaning and beyond. Bitter flavours are more challenging for babies to get used to than familiar flavours, like sweet (which they will have experienced with breast milk or formula). Some parents prefer to introduce a range of different fruits and vegetables initially, including single green vegetables alongside root vegetables and fruit. Remember, what you continue to offer is as important as what you start with.

**Q.** CAN YOU EXPLAIN THE DIFFERENCES BETWEEN BABY-LED WEANING AND PURÉES AND THEIR BENEFITS?

**A.** In short, purées tend to be considered a more 'traditional' weaning approach, where babies are given blended options via spoon by their parents, gradually progressing through different texture stages. Baby-led weaning focuses on offering safe family foods so the baby can self-feed from the beginning of weaning, and separate meals do not need to be made.

Baby-led weaning promotes self-feeding and encourages babies to explore different tastes and textures at their own pace. This approach fosters independence, fine motor skills development and a positive relationship with food. By offering whole foods from the family table, baby-led weaning simplifies meal preparation and encourages healthy eating habits.

Purées offer the benefit of controlling the texture and consistency of the food, making it easier for babies to swallow initially. They also allow parents to introduce a wide variety of flavours and nutrients in a more 'controlled' manner, catering to their baby's needs and preferences. However, your baby can still lead the approach, and opportunities to develop self-feeding skills and a positive relationship with food still exist.

Ultimately, the choice between purées and baby-led weaning depends on your baby, parenting style and family's preferences. Some parents find that combining both methods works best for their child, allowing them to reap the benefits of each approach while adapting to their baby's needs. Regardless of your chosen approach, the most critical aspect of weaning is to follow your baby's cues and provide a supportive and nurturing environment for exploring food. The end goal of both approaches is the same!

**Q.** WHAT ESSENTIAL WEANING TOOLS SHOULD I HAVE?

**A.** While you can be told that many items are a necessity during weaning, in reality, there are only a handful of essentials:

- A highchair is probably one of the most important decisions you'll make about weaning equipment. A supported eating position helps keep babies and children safe, supported and able to interact easily with their food. Choose an option ideally with an adjustable footrest (you need your feet to eat), a removable tray and which seats your child in a comfortable, upright position in which they can easily reach the food.
- Easy-to-grip cutlery is a great starting point. Ideally, this should be made from a material that is soft and easy to mouth on gums. As your baby develops, shorter-handled options with wider, easy-to-grasp handles can help your baby get to grips with using the cutlery themselves.

- You will need some bowls and plates to offer food (although the tray is also great!). Some parents prefer options that suction to the tray easily and materials that are easy to clean.
- During weaning, your baby will be messy (sorry!). Bibs help protect clothing, so choose a front-covering or an overall option.
- If you're introducing puréed or blended foods, you'll need a blender, but a hand or jug blender is fine.

**Q.** WHICH TYPE OF CUP IS BEST FOR BEGINNING WEANING, AND HOW DO I TEACH MY BABY TO DRINK FROM IT?

**A.** A small, open cup or unvalved sippy cup can be an excellent first cup for babies. It takes time to grasp cup drinking (a whole new skill), and your baby will rely on your modelling, lots of practice and some support initially to stabilise the cup at their mouth. Learning to use a cup takes time. Expect plenty of splashing, spills and spitting out. As your baby gets a little older, e.g. 8–9 months, you may also wish to introduce a weighted straw cup.

**Q.** CAN MY BABY HAVE TAP WATER, AND HOW MUCH WATER DO BABIES NEED?

**A.** In the UK, you can introduce your baby to tap water at 6 months of age. Before this, your baby should be offered cooled boiled water. Avoid bottled and/or mineral water unless these are identified as suitable for babies.

Babies will gradually increase the amount of water they accept as they become more proficient at cup drinking, so try not to worry too much about volumes initially. Fluids from their milk and food also contribute to their hydration needs.

**Q.** WHICH FOODS SHOULD I AVOID DURING EARLY WEANING, AND WHEN SHOULD I INTRODUCE THEM?

**A.** A range of foods need to be avoided during weaning. These include:
- Honey: this cannot be introduced until at least 12 months of age due to the risk of exposure to a bacteria that can cause a severe condition called infant botulism.
- Foods high in sugar: babies should not be offered foods high in sugar or that contain high amounts of added sugars (this includes any free sugars such as fruit concentrates and syrups). Guidance in the UK is that these foods are limited for babies and children under 2 years of age.

- Foods high in salt: babies under 12 months old should have no more than 1g of salt daily. Avoid high-salt foods, such as processed meats and crisps, and be mindful of portion sizes of salty foods, such as cheese and stocks.
- Foods that are a choking risk should be avoided for all babies and young children or else be adapted to be made safe (see below).
- Soft or loosely cooked eggs that do not have the British Lion Stamp, due to Salmonella risk.
- Rice drinks (cow's milk alternatives) should be avoided until around 5 years of age due to their naturally occurring arsenic levels.
- Raw or lightly cooked shellfish is considered a high risk of foodborne illness, so it should be avoided until your baby is at least 12 months old.
- Shark, swordfish and marlin are not common weaning foods in the UK, but should be avoided due to their mercury content, which can impact a baby's development.

**Q.** **WHAT ARE THE MAIN CHOKING HAZARDS FOR BABIES AND CHILDREN UNDER 4 YEARS?**

**A.** The most common foods are a size and/or texture that could easily block your child's airway. These include popcorn, whole nuts, spoonfuls of thick nut butter, whole grapes, large blueberries, cherry tomatoes, jelly cubes, marshmallows, toffee/sweets, chocolate eggs, sausages or hot dogs cut into rounds and raw chunks of hard fruits and vegetables, such as apples and carrot. While some of these foods can be adapted, for example by milling nuts, slicing sausages into fingers rather than rounds and cutting or grating fruits and vegetables appropriately, some, like popcorn, hard-boiled sweets and mini chocolate eggs, should be avoided entirely.

**Q.** **WHAT'S THE DIFFERENCE BETWEEN CHOKING AND GAGGING?**

**A.** Gagging and choking are easily confused – but are very different. Gagging is a protective mechanism that is very common for babies to experience during weaning. When a baby is gagging, they may have facial redness, retching, tongue thrusting (their tongue moving forward to remove the food), watering eyes and they will probably make lots of noise! Choking, on the other hand, is a more severe and potentially life-threatening situation in which the airway is blocked, preventing breathing. Signs of choking can be quiet, including a silent or weak cough, inability to breathe or speak, loss of colour from the face and/or lips and a panicked or distressed expression. It's crucial for parents and caregivers to understand the distinction between gagging and choking and to know how to respond appropriately in each situation.

If your baby is gagging, it's best to remain calm and allow them to work through it on their own. Intervening, for example, putting your fingers in their mouth or throat, may increase the risk of choking. Gagging is a natural part of learning to eat solid foods and is the body's way of preventing choking by pushing food forward in the mouth. However, if your baby is choking and unable to breathe or cough, immediate action is necessary to clear the airway and dislodge the obstruction, including emergency support.

Learning infant CPR and first aid techniques can give parents the confidence and skills to respond effectively in a choking emergency. Additionally, to reduce the risk of choking, ensure that the food offered to your baby is appropriate in size, texture and consistency.

**Q. WHEN SHOULD MY BABY GET UP TO THREE MEALS PER DAY?**

**A.** I am asked so often about babies' timeframes to reach this milestone! Each baby's progress through the first weeks and months of solids will differ. Most babies should get to three meals a day between 6½ to 9 months of age.

**Q. HOW DO I TEACH MY BABY TO USE CUTLERY?**

**A.** Cutlery skills take time, and I always reassure parents that it's common for babies and young children to use and choose their hands to eat! You can support cutlery skills in the following ways:

- Pre-load spoons and allow the baby to pick them up and bring them to their mouth (they may well miss them initially!).
- Role-modelling and eating with your child – they will watch you using cutlery and start to copy.
- Choosing ergonomic cutlery that is easier for your baby to hold and manipulate, such as those with wider, thicker handles.
- Using some gentle hand-over-hand help to encourage them to build skills like scooping with a spoon.

**Q. HOW DO I INTRODUCE ALLERGENIC FOODS, AND WHAT SIGNS OF AN ALLERGY SHOULD I LOOK FOR?**

**A.** Common food allergens should be introduced proactively during weaning, including cow's milk, eggs, wheat, soya, peanuts, tree nuts, fish, shellfish and sesame. I always recommend that parents introduce these one at a time, starting with small amounts of the allergen, for example ¼ teaspoon of loosened peanut butter, and gradually increase the amounts over consecutive days (or every second or third day if it's an allergen that may be more commonly associated with delayed food allergies, such as eggs, wheat, soya or milk). Introducing allergens in the morning can be helpful to allow time to monitor your baby throughout the day. Offer them on a day when your child is well and skin conditions such as eczema are well controlled. Once allergens are introduced, they should be maintained in your baby's diet.

Food allergy symptoms will depend on your baby's reaction to a food. There are two types of food allergy: immediate type (IgE mediated), where symptoms occur quickly after consuming a food, within minutes or up to 2 hours later, and delayed (non-IgE mediated), where symptoms happen 2–72 hours later.

Allergy symptoms can often affect more than one body system. These are the most common symptoms of a food allergy:

**Immediate (symptoms occur within minutes or up to 2 hours later)**

- **Skin**: hives (nettle rash, wheels), rash, itching, immediate eczema flare, redness and/or swelling.
- **Gut**: vomiting, diarrhoea, nausea.
- **Breathing**: sneezing, runny nose, coughing, wheezing, shortness of breath, hoarse cry.
- **Other:** floppiness, anaphylaxis (a life-threatening reaction that needs immediate medical attention).

**Delayed (symptoms occur 2–72 hours later)**

- **Skin:** Persistent eczema that does not improve with skin treatment (maybe widespread), as well as itching.
- **Gut:** reflux, vomiting, abdominal (tummy) pain, diarrhoea, constipation, excess mucus in poo, blood in poo.
- **Other:** refusing milk or food, slow growth.

If you suspect your child has symptoms of either type of food allergy, you should seek medical advice from your doctor. For any immediate reactions, especially anaphylaxis, please seek immediate emergency support.

 **WHY IS IT IMPORTANT FOR MY FAMILY TO EAT MEALS TOGETHER?**

 I understand it can be difficult to eat together, especially if your child's eating times are earlier or not in line with your usual schedule. Finding time for family meals is very well evidenced to support your child's acceptance of a variety of foods and has also been linked to a reduced risk of chronic diseases, improved academic performance and strengthened family bonds. Sharing meals allows for meaningful interactions and communication, fostering a sense of belonging and connection within the family. Additionally, children who regularly eat with their families are more likely to develop healthier eating habits and attitudes towards food. Prioritising family meals, even if it means adjusting schedules or making compromises, can have long-lasting benefits for children's and adults' overall health and well-being.

**Q.** HOW DO I CREATE A BALANCED PLATE FOR MY BABY, AND WHAT IS THE ROLE OF EACH FOOD GROUP?

**A.** Until a child reaches school age, they don't follow all the general 'healthy eating' dietary guidelines we have in place in the UK. This is because their nutritional needs are different. As a guide, building a balanced plate for your baby should look like this:

- One good iron-rich food, such as meat, poultry, oily fish, eggs or beans/legumes.
- One portion of fruit and/or vegetables (the more variety, the better).
- One energy-providing food, such as starchy carbohydrates and/or a higher fat food, such as pasta with olive oil or cream cheese, bread with butter or spread, potatoes and avocado, whole milk with cereal.

For young children (1–4 years) a balanced diet and plate looks like this:

5-A-DAY FRUIT AND VEGETABLES

5-A-DAY STARCHY FOODS

3-A-DAY DAIRY FOODS

2-A-DAY PROTEIN FOODS*
*3 PORTIONS IF CHILD IS VEGETARIAN

Each food group provides vital nutrients to support your baby or child's rapid growth and development. Protein and iron-rich foods support muscle growth, brain development and a healthy immune system. Fruits and vegetables provide essential vitamins, minerals, fibre and antioxidants that support overall health, immunity and digestive function. Carbohydrates are the body's primary energy source, fuelling physical activity and providing fibre and B vitamins for optimal metabolism and digestive health. Including dairy and fortified alternatives ensures adequate calcium intake, which is vital for bone health, teeth development and overall growth in children.

## Q. WHAT ARE YOUR BEST TIPS FOR INCREASING THE CALORIE CONTENT IN MY BABY'S FOOD?

**A.** Some babies may need extra energy in their diet, especially if there are concerns about their growth. It's also important to remember that all babies have high requirements for nutrients like fat, which should comprise 30–40 per cent of their energy intake. You can add extra energy to your baby's weaning diet by:

- Stirring oil, e.g. olive oil, through potatoes, pasta or rice.
- Roasting vegetables for sauces and soups or finger foods.
- Incorporating oily fish into the diet weekly.
- Adding options like nut and seed butter (or milled nuts/seeds) to porridge, cereals, yoghurts and bakes.
- Incorporating higher fat foods regularly into meals, e.g. eggs, avocado, oils and spreads, hummus, dairy and suitable alternatives and coconut.

## Q. HOW AND WHEN SHOULD I TRANSITION MY BABY TO COW'S MILK, AND WHAT ARE THE RECOMMENDED AMOUNTS?

**A.** Babies can have cow's milk in their food from 6 months of age and can be offered it as a drink from 12 months. When introduced as a drink at 12 months of age, you may titrate this (gradually add it) to your baby's current milk, whether that is breast milk or formula, or just start offering it in small amounts from a cup. It might take your child some time to get used to the taste, and some toddlers never accept cow's milk as a drink (which is OK!). From 12 months of age, ideally, your child should have no more than 350–400ml (12–14fl oz/1½ –1⅔ cups) milk per day or 2–3 portions of milk or dairy produce (e.g. milk, cheese, yoghurt). Excess intake of cow's milk as a drink in the toddler years can impact appetite, displace nutrients and increase the risk of some nutrient deficiencies, such as iron.

**Q.** WHAT ARE THE BEST DAIRY-FREE ALTERNATIVES TO COW'S MILK?

**A.** The best alternatives are those that help meet young children's high energy and nutrient needs. Ideally, I would encourage parents to choose a milk alternative with a nutritional composition similar to whole cow's milk. Most babies and young children should opt for an option based on either soya, oat, pea or coconut. The energy (calorie) content should be over 45–50 kcal/100ml (3½fl oz) and fortified with essential nutrients like calcium and iodine. Wherever possible, avoid sweetened options, milk alternatives labelled as organic (due to the lack of added vitamins and minerals) and nut-based milk alternatives, as the energy content is too low for growing babies and children. Rice milk alternatives should be avoided until 5 years of age.

**Q.** HOW CAN I KEEP MY BABY FROM THROWING FOOD ON THE FLOOR?

**A.** I'm afraid there is no magic wand here, and food throwing is something I tell parents to expect as part of a baby's development. Depending on your child's age, you can help manage food throwing by:

- Being mindful of how much food you're offering on the plate or tray – too much can cause some children to be overwhelmed.
- Checking in on meal timings and appetite – especially if your baby doesn't seem interested in food.
- Do not react! Keep calm and use positive language, such as, 'Oh no, your food is on the floor, but food stays on the table!'
- Ending the meal if food throwing persists and there is minimal interest in eating.
- Bringing your baby up to the table and removing their tray – especially over 12 months of age.

Breathe, and remember this phase will pass!

**Q.** DO YOU HAVE ANY TIPS FOR REDUCING STRESS DURING THE WEANING PROCESS?

**A.** It is important to normalise the fact that almost all parents feel some degree of stress during weaning. Feeding children is a very emotive topic, and awareness of the importance of child nutrition is growing, but with that can come an added layer of pressure. I would encourage parents to avoid comparing their baby's progress to others and instead think about what their child is doing and their next steps. Eating with your babies and children also helps you focus on your eating/food and reduces the pressure or risk of scrutinising everything they do at mealtimes. Finally, I think there is lots of focus on how much babies are eating, whereas what's often more important, especially across the first few months, is variety – not volume! Portion sizes don't exist for babies during weaning for a reason.

**Q.** **HOW CAN I EMBRACE THE POSITIVE ASPECTS OF MESSY EATING?**

**A.** Weaning can be challenging if you struggle with mess. I often ask parents to reframe mess as a necessary skill for learning. Getting messy during weaning helps babies develop the skills to eat and self-feed, build rich sensory experiences and not fear messiness themselves.

**Q.** **MY BABY SEEMS SLOW TO WEAN — IS THIS NORMAL?**

**A.** This is one of the biggest concerns that hits my inbox. It's important to remind parents that weaning isn't a race, and like any other aspect of development, children progress at their own speed. Many parents say that their 7–8-month-old baby still doesn't seem interested in food. I remind parents that babies at this stage have often only been developing these new skills for weeks (we don't expect babies to learn to walk in this time frame, for example!). Learning to eat is not just about how much food your baby consumes, but all the other skills they learn, from handling food to familiarising themselves with its smell and texture. If you're a parent in this position, please try not to 'fix it' and instead keep offering your baby opportunities to develop the skills and experience they need to eat food. If you need support, however, and something doesn't feel right, contact an experienced health professional.

## RESOURCES

Please refer to our Q&A section on page 10 for frequently asked questions about weaning. In addition to this, we would recommend visiting the Solid Starts website for comprehensive information on preparing food for babies and children, as well as the Food Standards Agency information sheet, which can be found here: https://foundationyears.org.uk

## RECIPE ICONS

Icons have been included next to all the recipes to help you understand at a glance which dishes are suitable for you and your baby's dietary needs. Where there is an option to swap an ingredient or tweak a recipe to make it suitable, that is also highlighted with the relevant icon.

 Egg-free

 Dairy-free option

 Vegan

 Egg-free option

 Vegetarian

 Vegan option

 Dairy-free

# HOW TO CUT FOOD FOR BABIES

| STRAWBERRIES | GRAPES | BLUEBERRIES | CARROT | BANANA | BROCCOLI |
| --- | --- | --- | --- | --- | --- |

**6 months+**
(big, ripe
and soft)

**9 months+**

**6 months+**
(flattened)

**6 months+**
(cooked)

**6 months+**

**6 months+**
(steamed florets)

**9 months+**
(sliced)

**18 months+**

**9 months+**
(flattened
a bit less)

**9 months+**
(cooked or
grated raw)

**9 months+**

**9 months+**
(steamed small
florets)

**24 months+**

**24 months+**

**24 months+**

**24 months+**
(raw, quartered)

**24 months+**

**12 months+**
(bite sized)

TOMATO    PEAS    PEANUTS    APPLE    AVOCADO

6 months+
(thin, smooth
peanut butter mixed
with food)

6 months+
(cooked halves)

6 months+

6 months+
(large wedges)

6 months+
(blended)

9 months+
(thin slices)

18 months+

9 months+

9 months+
(quartered
cherry tomatoes)

9 months+
(flattened)

12 months+
(smooth peanut butter
thinly spread on toast)

18 months+

24 months+

12 months+

5 years+

24 months+
(quartered)

# BREAKFAST

# HOMEMADE GRANOLA

We love snacking on a bowl of yoghurt topped with homemade granola! After realising how much added sugar store-bought options contain, I began making my own granola at home. I enjoy customising it with my favourite ingredients, always experimenting with new flavours!

    Makes: 1 medium jar (about 10 servings)  Prep: 5 minutes Cook: 30 minutes  Age: from 2 years

150g (5½oz/1½ cups) porridge oats

60g (2oz/½ cup) raw unsalted nuts of your choice, such as almonds, walnuts or cashews, roughly chopped

40g (1½oz/¼ cup) seeds of your choice, such as sunflower or pumpkin, roughly chopped (see Tip)

a pinch of ground cinnamon

2 tablespoons virgin coconut oil

3½ tablespoons maple syrup

2 tablespoons raisins (optional)

1. Preheat your oven to 140°C/110°C fan/275°F/ gas 1 and line a baking tray with baking paper.

2. Put the oats, nuts, seeds and cinnamon into a large bowl and stir well.

3. Put the coconut oil and maple syrup into a pan and gently warm, just enough to melt the coconut oil.

4. Pour the coconut oil mixture over the oat mixture, then stir well to combine.

5. Spread the mixture evenly onto the prepared baking tray and press down with a spatula to form clusters.

6. Bake in the oven for 25–30 minutes until golden brown, stirring halfway through to ensure it cooks evenly.

7. Remove from the oven and stir in the raisins, if using. Allow to cool completely before transferring to an airtight container.

8. Buon appetito!

 **STORAGE** Store in airtight container for up to 1 month at room temperature or for up to 2 months in the fridge.

**TIPS** Feel free to replace the raisins with chopped dates or dried apricots.

For smaller children, nuts and seeds must be chopped finely so that they do not pose a choking hazard. You can do this in a food processor – pulse for 30 seconds, or until chopped to your liking.

# BAKED OATS

The girls adore it when I make baked oats for them in the morning as it's like having cake for breakfast! You'll be surprised by how easy it is – just blend everything together, bake and enjoy!

    Serves: 2 children  Prep: 5 minutes Cook: 20 minutes  Age: from 6 months

**NOTE: don't add the chocolate for children under 2 years old**

60g (2oz) peeled, cored and thickly sliced crisp eating apple, such as Pink Lady or Gala

170ml (5¾fl oz/¾ cup) whole cow's milk or plant-based milk alternative

80g (2¾oz/¾ cup) porridge oats

1 teaspoon baking powder

1 handful of dark chocolate chips

1. Preheat the oven to 180°C/160°C fan/350°F/ gas 4.

2. In a blender, combine the apple slices and milk. Pulse until smooth.

3. Add the oats and baking powder and blend again until smooth.

4. Pour the batter into a 12 x 16cm (5 x 6½ inch) baking dish or two smaller ones and sprinkle with the chocolate chips.

5. Bake in the oven for 20 minutes until golden on top.

6. Remove from the oven and allow to cool slightly before serving.

7. Buon appetito!

 **STORAGE** Cover and store in the fridge for up to 3 days.

**TIPS** If you don't have apples, use a small, ripe banana instead.

For children over 2 years old and adults, you can add 1 teaspoon maple syrup or honey to the batter.

You can also bake the oats in two individual baking dishes if you prefer.

# OVERNIGHT OATS FOUR WAYS

Overnight oats are the ultimate breakfast hack! They only take a couple of minutes to throw together. I usually make four servings in one go so that they are ready to go on busy mornings. I love adding nut butters to overnight oats – young children need plenty of energy from fat in their diet and options like these are a great source of healthy fats and fibre. Equally, chia seeds are a nutritional powerhouse of nutrients, from fibre to calcium.

    Serves: 2 children  Prep: 5 minutes, plus overnight soaking time  Age: from 6 months

## APPLE PIE

1 crisp eating apple, such as Pink Lady or Gala, peeled, cored and grated

60g (2oz/⅔ cup) porridge oats

100ml (3½fl oz/scant ½ cup) whole cow's milk or plant-based milk alternative

100ml (3½fl oz/scant ½ cup) Greek yoghurt or dairy-free Greek -style yoghurt

1 tablespoon chia seeds

1 teaspoon smooth almond butter (optional)

pinch of ground cinnamon

## PEANUT BUTTER AND BANANA

1 small ripe banana, mashed

60g (2oz/⅔ cup) porridge oats

100ml (3½fl oz/scant ½ cup) whole cow's milk or plant-based milk alternative

100ml (3½fl oz/½ cup) Greek yoghurt or dairy-free Greek-style yoghurt

1 tablespoon chia seeds

1 teaspoon smooth peanut butter (optional)

**TIPS** If your almond butter is a bit too thick to mix in easily, blend it with the milk first before stirring it into the rest of the ingredients.

**TIPS** If your peanut butter is a bit too thick to mix in easily, blend it with the milk first before stirring it into the rest of the ingredients.

# CARROT CAKE

50g (1¾oz) carrot, peeled and grated

60g (2oz/⅔ cup) porridge oats

100ml (3½fl oz/scant ½ cup) whole cow's milk or plant-based milk alternative

100ml (3½fl oz/scant ½ cup) Greek yoghurt or dairy-free Greek-style yoghurt

1 tablespoon chia seeds

1 teaspoon ground walnuts or almond butter (optional)

pinch of ground cinnamon

**TIPS** For children over two years and adults, you can add a small handful of roughly chopped raisins.

# STRAWBERRY CHEESECAKE

3–4 strawberries, chopped

60g (2oz/⅔ cup) porridge oats

100ml (3½fl oz/scant ½ cup) whole cow's milk or plant-based milk alternative

80ml (2¾fl oz/⅓ cup) Greek yoghurt or dairy-free Greek-style yoghurt

3 tablespoons cream cheese or mascarpone

1 tablespoon chia seeds

1. Combine all the ingredients in a bowl and mix well.
2. Transfer to two small airtight containers, then rest in the fridge overnight.
3. Enjoy the next morning! Buon appetito!

 **STORAGE** Store in an airtight container in the fridge for up to 3 days.

**TIPS** For children over two years and adults, you can add 1 tablespoon maple syrup or honey for a touch of sweetness.

Carrot Cake
Overnight Oats

Strawberry
Cheesecake
Overnight Oats

Apple Pie
Overnight Oats

Peanut Butter
and Banana
Overnight Oats

# BLUEBERRY BANANA PORRIDGE

This recipe is a reminder of the special mornings when Mattia would wake up early for Kate, to make their favourite quick breakfast. Kate loved it so much that she'd eat it all up every time. It was their little ritual: one bowl for her and one for Mattia!

    Serves: 1 child     Prep: 5 minutes Cook: 5 minutes     Age: from 6 months

40g (1½oz/⅓ cup) porridge oats

120ml (4fl oz/½ cup) whole cow's milk or plant-based milk alternative

30g (1oz/¼ cup) frozen blueberries

½ small ripe banana

1. Put the oats, milk and blueberries into a saucepan over a medium heat and bring to the boil.

2. Reduce to a simmer and cook, stirring regularly, for 5 minutes, or until the porridge is thick and creamy.

3. Stir through the mashed banana.

4. Allow to cool slightly before serving.

5. Buon appetito!

 **STORAGE** Store leftovers in an airtight container in the fridge for up to 2 days, or freeze for up to 3 months. Defrost in the fridge overnight. Reheat in a pan over a low-medium heat with a splash of milk or water if needed.

 **TIPS** Porridge can sometimes be tricky for babies to manage during baby-led weaning. To encourage self-feeding, pre-load spoons and offer them to your baby, waiting for them to grab them.

Blueberry Banana
Porridge

Carrot Cake
Porridge

# CARROT CAKE PORRIDGE

I only discovered porridge when I arrived in London because it's not well-known in Italy. Perhaps in recent years, thanks to social media, it has become more popular, but it's not as common to eat it there as it is here. I loved it from the start and enjoy experimenting with different versions and combinations. This is one of the porridges I've always loved preparing for my kids because it's a nutritional boost, perfect for starting the day on the right foot.

    Serves: 1 child    Prep: 5 minutes Cook: 8 minutes    Age: from 6 months

1 crisp eating apple, peeled, cored and grated

1 small carrot, peeled and grated

40g (1½oz/⅓ cup) porridge oats

120ml (4fl oz/½ cup) whole cow's milk or plant-based milk alternative, plus extra as needed

1 teaspoon ground almonds (optional)

a pinch of ground cinnamon (optional)

1. Combine all the ingredients in a saucepan over a medium heat and bring to the boil.

2. Reduce to a simmer and cook, stirring regularly, for 8–10 minutes, or until the porridge is thick and creamy, adding a little more milk if necessary.

3. Allow to cool slightly before serving.

4. Buon appetito!

 **STORAGE** Store leftovers in an airtight container in the fridge for up to 2 days, or freeze for up to 3 months. Defrost in the fridge overnight. Reheat in a pan over a low-medium heat with a splash of milk or water if needed.

 **TIPS** Porridge can sometimes be tricky for babies to manage during baby-led weaning. To encourage self-feeding, pre-load spoons and offer them to your baby, waiting for them to grab them.

BREAKFAST

# EGG-FREE BANANA PEANUT BUTTER PANCAKES

These banana pancakes are not only egg-free, making them perfect for those with egg allergies, but they're also dairy-free and vegan! I've included peanut butter in the recipe to give your little one an added boost of iron and protein. However, if your child has an allergy, feel free to leave it out.

    Makes: 10–12 pancakes  Prep: 5 minutes Cook: 10 minutes  Age: from 6 months

1 small ripe banana

60g (2oz/⅔ cup) porridge oats

100ml (3½fl oz/scant ½ cup) whole cow's milk or plant-based milk alternative

2 heaped tablespoons smooth peanut butter

1 teaspoon chia seeds (optional)

½ teaspoon baking powder

virgin coconut oil or unsalted butter, for frying

1. Put all the ingredients into a food processor and blend until a smooth batter forms.

2. Heat a little coconut oil or butter in a frying pan over a medium heat, then drop in 1–2 tablespoons of the batter.

3. Cook for 3 minutes until bubbles form on the top and the edges are dry. Flip and cook for 3 minutes until browned. Repeat with the remaining batter.

4. Let the pancakes cool slightly before serving.

5. Buon appetito!

**STORAGE** Store the cooled pancakes in an airtight container in the fridge for up to 3 days. Freeze the pancakes individually on a baking sheet, then transfer to a freezer bag and freeze for up to 3 months. Defrost in the fridge overnight. Reheat from frozen or chilled in the toaster or microwave until warmed through.

# CARROT AND BANANA PANCAKES

I adore pancakes because they're so versatile and easy for little hands to grab. These pancakes are naturally sweetened with banana and carrot and can easily be made egg-free.

   Makes: 10–12 pancakes  Prep: 5 minutes Cook: 10 minutes  Age: from 6 months

60g (2oz) ripe banana

40g (1½oz) carrot, peeled and roughly chopped

1 medium egg or chia egg (see Tip)

100ml (3½fl oz/scant ½ cup) whole cow's milk or plant-based milk alternative

90g (3¼oz/scant 1 cup) porridge oats

½ teaspoon baking powder

1 teaspoon smooth almond butter (optional)

virgin coconut oil or unsalted butter, for frying

1. Put the banana, carrot, egg and milk into a food processor and blend until smooth.

2. Add the oats, baking powder and almond butter, if using, then blend again until a smooth batter forms.

3. Heat a little coconut oil or butter in a frying pan over medium heat, then drop in 1–2 tablespoons of the batter.

4. Cook for 3 minutes until bubbles form on the top and the edges are dry. Flip and cook for 3 minutes until browned. Repeat with the remaining batter.

5. Let the pancakes cool slightly before serving.

6. Buon appetito!

 **STORAGE** Store the cooled pancakes in an airtight container in the fridge for up to 3 days. Freeze the pancakes individually on a baking sheet, then transfer to a freezer bag and freeze for up to 3 months. Defrost in the fridge overnight. Reheat from frozen or chilled in the toaster or microwave until warmed through.

 **TIPS** To make the recipe egg-free, use a chia egg: mix 1 tablespoon chia seeds with 3 tablespoons water, allow to sit for 5 minutes, then use in place of the egg. Let the mixture rest for 10 minutes before cooking.

You may need to add a little more milk or water if using a chia egg as the mixture will become denser.

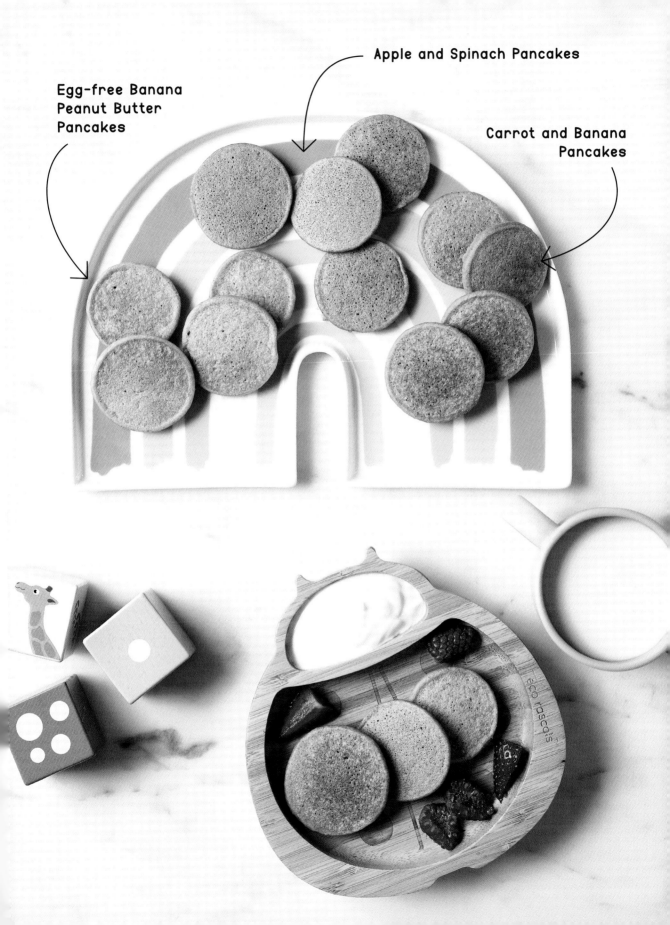

Egg-free Banana Peanut Butter Pancakes

Apple and Spinach Pancakes

Carrot and Banana Pancakes

# APPLE AND SPINACH PANCAKES

Pancakes are a staple in our household, especially for baby-led weaning – as you can see from the abundance of pancake recipes in this book! Ever since my girls were little, I've made it my mission to incorporate vegetables into their meals, and these pancakes are an easy and delicious way to introduce veggies into your child's diet – my kids have affectionately named them 'monster pancakes' and happily devour them for breakfast and snacks alike.

   Makes: 10–12 pancakes   Prep: 5 minutes Cook: 10 minutes   Age: from 6 months

1 small crisp eating apple, peeled, cored and roughly chopped

1 handful of spinach leaves

120ml (4fl oz/½ cup) whole cow's milk or plant-based milk alternative

1 medium egg or chia egg (see page 38)

100g (3½oz/1 cup) porridge oats

½ teaspoon baking powder

virgin coconut oil or unsalted butter, for frying

1. Put the apple, spinach, milk and egg into a food processor and blend until very smooth.

2. Add the oats and baking powder, then blend again until a smooth batter forms.

3. Heat a little coconut oil or butter in a frying pan over a medium heat, then drop in 1–2 tablespoons of the batter.

4. Cook for 3 minutes until bubbles form on the top and the edges are dry. Flip and cook for a further 3 minutes until browned. Repeat with the remaining batter.

5. Let the pancakes cool slightly before serving.

6. Buon appetito!

 **TIPS**   If you don't have an apple, you can use a banana instead.

You may need to add a little more milk or water if using a chia egg as the mixture will become denser.

You can store a bag of baby spinach in the freezer to use in smoothies and pancakes. Freezing it retains the nutrients but removes any 'green' flavour, which is handy! You also don't have to worry about it going bad before you have time to use it all.

# SWEET POTATO PANCAKES

These pancakes are a simple way to introduce your child to sweet potatoes. Made with just a handful of wholesome ingredients, they're incredibly soft and perfect for kids of all ages.

   Makes: 8 pancakes    Prep: 5 minutes   Cook: 10 minutes    Age: from 6 months

100g (3½oz) sweet potato, peeled and roughly chopped

1 medium egg

2 tablespoons wholemeal or plain flour

½ teaspoon baking powder

virgin coconut oil or unsalted butter, for frying

1. Steam the sweet potato over a gentle heat until soft, then set aside to cool. Once cooled, weigh out 80g (2¾oz) of the potato (any leftovers can be discarded or saved for later use).

2. Put the sweet potato into a bowl and mash with a fork, then add the remaining ingredients and mix until well combined.

3. Heat a little coconut oil or butter in a frying pan over a medium-high heat, then drop in 1–2 tablespoons of the batter to make each pancake.

4. Cook for 3 minutes until firm enough to slide a spatula underneath without the pancakes breaking, then flip and cook for a further 3 minutes until golden brown. Repeat with the remaining batter.

5. Let the pancakes cool slightly before serving.

6. Buon appetito!

**STORAGE** Store the cooled pancakes in an airtight container in the fridge for up to 3 days. Freeze the pancakes individually on a baking sheet, then transfer to a freezer bag for up to 3 months. Defrost in the fridge overnight. Reheat from frozen or chilled in the toaster or microwave until warmed through.

# APPLE AND GREEK YOGHURT PANCAKES

Pancakes are undoubtedly the easiest and most convenient breakfast or snack option I whip up for my daughters. They're perfect for on-the-go mornings as well. With no additional sweeteners, the natural sweetness of the apples determines the flavour of these pancakes.

   Makes: 10–12 pancakes  Prep: 5 minutes Cook: 10 minutes  Age: from 6 months

1 crisp eating apple, peeled, cored and roughly chopped

60ml (2fl oz/¼ cup) Greek yoghurt or dairy-free Greek-style yoghurt

1 medium egg or chia egg (see page 38)

60g (2oz/⅔ cup) porridge oats

½ teaspoon baking powder

virgin coconut oil or unsalted butter, for frying

1. Put the apple, yoghurt and egg into a food processor and blend until smooth.

2. Add the oats and baking powder, then blend again until a smooth batter forms.

3. Heat a little coconut oil or butter in a frying pan over a medium heat, then drop in 1–2 tablespoons of batter.

4. Cook for 3 minutes until bubbles form on the top and the edges are dry. Flip and cook for a further 3 minutes until browned. Repeat with the remaining batter.

5. Let the pancakes cool slightly before serving.

6. Buon appetito!

 **STORAGE** Store the cooled pancakes in an airtight container in the fridge for up to 3 days. Freeze individually on a baking sheet, then transfer to a freezer bag and freeze for up to 3 months. Defrost in the fridge overnight. Reheat from frozen or chilled in the microwave until warmed through.

 **TIPS** Ensure the apples are well blended to avoid any large chunks in the batter.

You may need to add a little more yoghurt or water if using a chia egg as the mixture will become denser.

Sweet Potato Pancakes

Apple and Greek Yoghurt Pancakes

Grape Pancakes

# GRAPE PANCAKES

Long-time followers of my Instagram page will be aware of my love for pancake experiments, especially when my girls were little. I love how you can just blend together all the nutritious ingredients and – voilà – your child has a healthy, nourishing breakfast!

   Makes: 10 pancakes  Prep: 5 minutes Cook: 10 minutes  Age: from 6 months

120g (4¼oz) seedless grapes

1 medium egg or chia egg (see page 38)

3½ tablespoons whole cow's milk or plant-based milk alternative

80g (2¾oz/¾ cup) porridge oats

30g (1oz/¼ cup) wholemeal or plain flour

½ teaspoon baking powder

virgin coconut oil or unsalted butter, for frying

1.  Put the grapes, egg and milk into a food processor and blend until smooth.

2.  Add the oats, flour and baking powder, then blend again until a smooth batter forms.

3.  Heat a little coconut oil or butter in a frying pan over a medium heat, then drop in 1–2 tablespoons of the batter and use a spoon to spread out the mixture a little.

4.  Cook for 2–3 minutes until bubbles form on the top and the edges are dry. Flip and cook for a further 2–3 minutes until browned. Repeat with the remaining batter.

5.  Let the pancakes cool slightly before serving.

6.  Buon appetito!

 **STORAGE** Store the cooled pancakes in an airtight container in the fridge for up to 3 days. Freeze the pancakes individually on a baking sheet, then transfer to a freezer bag and freeze for up to 3 months. Defrost in the fridge overnight. Reheat in the toaster or microwave until warmed through (you can also reheat the pancakes from frozen in the microwave).

 **TIPS** Ensure the grapes are well blended to avoid large chunks in the batter, which could affect the texture of the pancakes.

You may need to add a little more milk or water if using a chia egg as the mixture will become denser.

# EGG-FREE FRENCH TOAST

This egg-free French toast has been a breakfast staple since the girls were little, adding some variety to our mornings. When they were younger, I used to serve it with Greek yoghurt and fruit. Now that they're older, they love it with maple syrup for dipping and a simple side of fruit, and so do I!

    **Serves:** 2 children  **Prep:** 5 minutes **Cook:** 10 minutes  **Age:** from 6 months

1 small ripe banana

80ml (2¾fl oz/⅓ cup) whole cow's milk or plant-based milk alternative

1 tablespoon chia seeds or flaxseeds

a pinch of ground cinnamon or a drop of vanilla extract (optional)

2 slices of bread

virgin coconut oil or unsalted butter, for frying

1. Combine all the ingredients except the bread in a food processor and blend until smooth, ensuring the chia seeds or flaxseeds have completely broken down so there is no discernible seed texture.

2. Transfer the mixture to a shallow bowl wide enough to hold a slice of bread. Let it sit for about 10 minutes to firm up.

3. Melt a generous amount of the coconut oil or butter in a frying pan over a medium-high heat.

4. Dip each side of the bread into the batter mixture and leave to soak for 10 seconds.

5. Transfer the bread to the pan and cook for 2–3 minutes on each side, or until golden brown. Add more butter or oil to the pan as needed.

6. Cut the French toast into sticks to serve.

7. Buon appetito!

 **STORAGE** Store in an airtight container in the fridge for up to 2 days, or freeze for up to 3 months. Reheat from chilled or frozen in the toaster until warmed through.

 **TIPS** For best results, use 2-day-old bread to prevent the French toast from becoming soggy.

If the bread is too soft, lightly toast it before dipping it into the mixture.

# BLUEBERRY AND BANANA FRENCH TOAST

Introduce your little one to a world of flavour with this simple French toast recipe. Ideal for weaning babies and toddlers, it's finger food fun that's both tasty and nutritious!

  Makes: 2–3 slices  Prep: 5 minutes Cook: 10 minutes  Age: from 6 months

1 small ripe banana

4–5 blueberries, halved

2 tablespoons whole cow's milk or plant-based milk alternative

1 medium egg

1 tablespoon smooth peanut butter (optional)

2–3 slices of bread

virgin coconut oil or unsalted butter, for frying

1. In a shallow bowl, mash the banana and blueberries together.

2. Add the milk, egg and peanut butter, if using. Mix well until combined.

3. Heat a little coconut oil or butter in a frying pan over a medium-high heat.

4. Dip each side of the bread into the batter, pressing the blueberry pieces into the bread, and leave to soak for about 10 seconds.

5. Transfer the bread to the pan and cook for 2–3 minutes on each side, or until golden brown. Add more butter or oil to the pan as needed.

6. Cut the French toast into sticks or squares to serve.

7. Buon appetito!

 **STORAGE** Store in an airtight container in the fridge for up to 2 days, or freeze for up to 3 months. Reheat from chilled or frozen in the toaster until warmed through.

 **TIPS** For best results, use two-day-old bread to prevent the French toast from becoming soggy.

I added peanut butter for a nutritional boost – you can substitute it with any nut or seed butter, or you can leave it out entirely.

# PEANUT BUTTER AND JAM BANANA ROLL UPS

Start your day with something fun! Quick, easy and a hit with the kids, these are one of my daughter Kate's favourite breakfasts, and a must-have in our house at least once a week. They are perfect for busy mornings.

    Serves: 1 child    Prep: 5 minutes   Cook: 5 minutes    Age: 9 months

1 slice of bread, crusts removed

1 small ripe banana

smooth peanut butter (or any nut or seed butter you like)

low-sugar strawberry jam (see Tip)

virgin coconut oil or unsalted butter, for frying

1. Use a rolling pin to roll out and flatten the bread.

2. Spread a thin layer of peanut butter and jam on top, then place the banana along one edge of the bread. Roll it up, trimming off any banana that protrudes from the bread.

3. Heat a little coconut oil or butter in a frying pan over a medium heat and fry the roll for 5 minutes until golden brown all over.

4. Slice into pieces using a sharp knife.

5. Buon appetito!

 **TIPS** If you want to use homemade jam, try mine on page 172. This is ideal for babies under 1 year old, as it contains no sugar.

Chia Jam

# BREAKFAST EGG MUFFIN

Busy parents, I've got you covered! These muffins are quick to make, delicious and packed with veggies. I always plan to make them ahead for easy mornings all week, but they disappear before the day's end!

 VEGETARIAN  Makes: 6 muffins 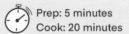 Prep: 5 minutes Cook: 20 minutes  Age: from 6 months

3 large eggs

30g (1oz/⅓ cup) grated Cheddar cheese

10g (½oz) spinach leaves, roughly chopped

2 cherry tomatoes, thinly sliced

1–2 tablespoons grated Parmesan cheese, for sprinkling

1. Preheat the oven to 180°C/160°C fan/350°F/gas 4 and line a six-hole muffin tin with muffin liners.

2. Put the eggs, cheese and spinach into a bowl and mix well.

3. Divide the mixture among the muffin liners, then top each muffin with a slice of cherry tomato and a sprinkle of Parmesan.

4. Bake in the oven for 20–25 minutes, or until the muffins are golden on top.

5. Remove from the oven and allow to cool slightly before serving as the cherry tomato on top can be very hot.

6. Buon appetito!

 **STORAGE** Store the cooled muffins in an airtight container in the fridge for up to 3 days, or freeze for up to 3 months. Defrost in the fridge overnight. To reheat, preheat the oven to 160°C/140°C fan/325°F/gas 2 and warm the muffins for 5–10 minutes, or until heated through.

 **TIPS** You can make these egg muffins in a mini muffin tin if you like – perfect for little hands! They will only need to bake for 10–15 minutes.

# BLUEBERRY BANANA FRITTERS

Bananas are always a staple in our home. I love how their natural sweetness can brighten up snacks and breakfasts. Want to know something about me? I rarely eat bananas as they are because I'm not a huge fan, but I absolutely love using them in cooking!

    Makes: 3 fritters

 Prep: 5 minutes
Cook: 5 minutes

 Age: from 6 months

60g (2oz) overripe banana

6 blueberries, cut in half

30g (1oz/¼ cup) oat flour (see Tip)

virgin coconut oil, for frying

1. Mash the banana in a bowl, then add the blueberries and oat flour, mixing gently until well combined.

2. Heat a generous amount of coconut oil in a non-stick frying pan over a low-medium heat.

3. Drop 1 tablespoon of the batter onto the pan for each fritter, using a spoon to spread out the mixture.

4. Fry the fritters for 2–3 minutes on each side until golden brown.

5. Let them cool slightly before serving, as the blueberries can be hot.

6. Buon appetito!

 **STORAGE** Store the cooled fritters in an airtight container in the fridge for up to 3 days. Freeze the fritters on a baking sheet, then transfer to a freezer bag and freeze for up to 3 months. Reheat from frozen in a lightly greased frying pan over a medium heat or in the microwave until warmed through.

 **TIPS** You can make oat flour at home by blending oats in a food processor until fine. So simple!

If your little one doesn't like blueberries, you can easily substitute them with chopped strawberries.

Blueberry
Banana
Fritters

Apple
Fritters

# APPLE FRITTERS

I love apple fritters for baby-led weaning because they offer a simple and delicious way to introduce apples to little ones right from their early days.

  Makes: 3 fritters  Prep: 5 minutes Cook: 5 minutes  Age: from 6 months

1 crisp eating apple, peeled, cored and grated

1 small egg

3 tablespoons porridge oats

a pinch of ground cinnamon (optional, but recommended for extra flavour)

virgin coconut oil or unsalted butter, for frying

1. Combine all the ingredients in a bowl and mix well until thoroughly combined.

2. Heat a generous amount of coconut oil or butter in a non-stick frying pan over low-medium heat, then drop in 1 tablespoon of the apple mixture for each fritter. Lightly press down with the back of the spoon to form a fritter shape.

3. Fry for 2–3 minutes on each side, or until golden brown and cooked through.

4. Remove the fritters from the pan and place on kitchen paper to drain any excess oil and allow to cool slightly.

5. Buon appetito!

 **STORAGE** Store the cooled fritters in an airtight container in the fridge for up to 2 days. Freeze individually on a baking sheet, then transfer to a freezer bag and freeze for up to 3 months. Reheat from frozen in a lightly greased frying pan over a low heat or in the microwave until warmed through.

 **TIPS** I recommend making a small test fritter first to check the temperature of the pan. If the outside scorches and the inside is still raw, then reduce the heat.

# CHOCOLATE SPREAD

My daughter Kate always loved shop-bought chocolate spread, but I couldn't help feeling guilty seeing her eat something so processed. I was determined to create a healthier alternative that still delivered the chocolatey joy she adored. Now, here we are with a recipe that's become Kate and Grace's new favourite! We love slathering this homemade spread on toast, swirling it into porridge and enjoying the peace of mind that comes from knowing exactly what's in it. Just 15 minutes of simple preparation leads to delicious, homemade goodness that's so much healthier than anything you'd find in the shops.

    Makes: 1 small jar  Prep: 15 minutes  Age: 12 months

30g (1oz) coconut sugar or light brown soft sugar

200g (7oz/1½ cups) roasted blanched hazelnuts

10g (⅓oz) raw cacao powder

1. Put the sugar into a food processor and blend to a powder.

2. Add the hazelnuts and blend for about 8–10 minutes until creamy. You will likely need to scrape the sides of the bowl down a few times. At first it will have a paste consistency, but eventually the oil will be released from the hazelnuts and it will become a creamy nut butter.

3. Add the cacao and blend again.

4. Transfer to an airtight jar.

5. Buon appetito!

 **STORAGE**  Store in the fridge for 2–3 weeks.

**TIPS**  You will need to use a high-powered food processor for this recipe otherwise it won't be that smooth.

# SO SIMPLE CRÊPES

At home, we often enjoy crêpes for breakfast, even on busy mornings. They're quick to make and everyone can fill them the way they like. Mattia and the girls prefer theirs with melted cheese, while I enjoy mine with jam. They're also a fun idea for dinner – we love them with grated cheese or grilled courgettes and cheese. Just prepare the crêpes and let everyone customise their own!

  VEGETARIAN · DAIRY-FREE OPTION

 Makes: 5 crêpes

Prep: 5 minutes
Cook: 10 minutes

 Age: from 6 months

1 medium egg

80g (2¾oz/⅔ cup) plain, wholemeal or white spelt flour

160ml (5½fl oz/⅔ cup) whole cow's milk or plant-based milk alternative

extra virgin olive oil or unsalted butter, for frying

**FILLING OPTIONS**

jam (see my strawberry jam on page 172)

chocolate spread (see my recipe on page 55)

smooth peanut butter

Greek yoghurt

fresh berries

grated cheese

1. Combine all the ingredients in a bowl or food processor and whisk or blend to form a smooth batter.

2. Heat a little oil or butter in a non-stick frying pan over medium heat, then drop in a small amount of batter and tilt it with a circular motion to coat the surface of the pan evenly.

3. Cook for 1–2 minutes until the top of the crêpe is no longer wet and the bottom has turned light brown. Use a spatula to loosen the crêpe, then flip it and cook for a further 1–2 minutes until light brown on the other side.

4. Repeat with the remaining batter.

5. Serve the crêpes with your favourite fillings.

6. Buon appetito!

 **STORAGE** Store the cooled crêpes covered with cling film in the fridge for up to 2 days. Freeze the crêpes layered between baking paper for up to 2 months. Reheat from chilled or frozen in a pan over a medium heat until warmed through.

 **TIPS** I use a 20cm (8 inch) pan; if you use a bigger one, you will have fewer crêpes.

Chocolate
Spread

# BANANA AND OAT WAFFLES

Waffles make a wonderful snack or breakfast for little ones. Their shape makes them easy to cut into fingers, which is ideal for baby-led weaning. I serve them with plain yoghurt, fruit and a touch of maple syrup for a fancy breakfast, or simply plain as a snack or lunchbox filler. Don't have a waffle maker? No problema! You can use this batter to make pancakes instead!

   **Serves:** 2 children  **Prep: 5 minutes** **Cook: 10 minutes**  **Age: from** 6 months

1 small ripe banana

1 small egg

40g (1½oz/generous ⅓ cup) porridge oats

virgin coconut oil or unsalted butter, for greasing and frying

1. Preheat a waffle maker and lightly grease it.

2. Put the banana, egg and oats into a food processor and pulse until they form a smooth batter.

3. Spoon the batter into the waffle maker.

4. Cook the waffles according to your waffle maker's instructions until golden.

5. Let the waffles cool slightly before serving.

6. Buon appetito!

 **STORAGE** Store the cooled waffles in an airtight container in the fridge for up to 2 days, or freeze for up to 3 months. Reheat from chilled or frozen in the toaster until warmed through.

 **TIPS** Be sure to preheat your waffle maker. If you don't, the exterior of the waffle won't crisp up properly.

# BREAKFAST CAKE

Who says you can't enjoy cake for breakfast? This simple breakfast cake brings together the best of both worlds – cake and pancakes! It is made with everyday kitchen ingredients that you likely already have on hand, and the best part is that you can customise it with your favourite toppings, whether that's juicy fresh berries or indulgent chocolate chips.

  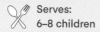 Serves: 6–8 children 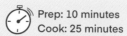 Prep: 10 minutes Cook: 25 minutes  Age: from 6 months

**NOTE: don't add the chocolate or sugar for children under 2 years old**

1 overripe banana

3 medium eggs

180ml (6fl oz/¾ cup) whole cow's milk or plant-based milk alternative

200g (7oz/1⅔ cups) self-raising flour (see Tip to make your own)

1 teaspoon baking powder

4 tablespoons coconut sugar or light brown soft sugar (optional)

1 handful of berries, such as chopped strawberries, blueberries or raspberries, or chocolate chips (optional)

unsalted butter, for greasing

1. Preheat the oven to 180°C/160°C fan/350°F/ gas 4 and lightly grease a 26 x 18cm (10 x 7 inch) baking dish with butter.

2. Mash the banana in a large bowl, then add the eggs and milk and mix well.

3. Add the flour, baking powder and sugar, if using, and stir until combined.

4. Pour the batter into the prepared baking dish and top with the berries or chocolate chips, if using.

5. Bake in the oven for 25–30 minutes until a skewer inserted into the centre comes out clean.

6. Remove from the oven and allow to cool slightly before serving.

7. Buon appetito!

 **STORAGE**  Store in an airtight container for up to 4 days, or freeze for up to 3 months. Defrost in the fridge overnight.

Warm the cake up in a low oven before serving, if desired.

**TIPS**   If you use a larger or smaller baking dish, you may need to adjust the cooking time accordingly.

To make your own self-raising flour, mix 360g (12½oz/scant 3 cups) plain flour with 4½ teaspoons baking powder and ¾ teaspoon salt. Use the required amount for this recipe and store the remainder for future baking.

# LUNCH AND DINNER

# CREAMY PEA SOUP

More from my unexpected love story with peas! As you've probably noticed, peas are my go-to green vegetable protein! The nutritional benefits of the humble pea are often overlooked. Just 40g (1½oz) provides about 10 per cent of a toddler's daily iron requirement, alongside a good dose of gut-friendly fibre. Peas are versatile, convenient and surprisingly tasty – that's why this recipe had to make it into my book. Can you believe I used to despise peas before I turned 25?

    Serves: 4 children     Prep: 10 minutes Cook: 25 minutes     Age: from 6 months

2 tablespoons extra virgin olive oil

50g (1¾oz) onion, chopped

350g (12oz/2⅓ cups) frozen peas

100g (3½oz) floury potatoes, peeled and chopped

350ml (12fl oz/1½ cups) boiling water

1 low-salt vegetable stock cube

grated Parmesan cheese, to serve (optional)

1. Heat the oil in a saucepan over a medium-high heat, then add the onion and sauté for 5–7 minutes until softened and golden.

2. Add the peas, potatoes, boiling water and stock cube. Stir well and bring to the boil.

3. Reduce the heat, cover and simmer for 20–25 minutes, or until the peas and potatoes are soft.

4. Remove from the heat and use a hand-held blender to purée the soup until smooth and creamy.

5. Serve with grated Parmesan on top, if desired.

6. Buon appetito!

 **STORAGE** Store in the fridge for up to 2 days, or freeze for up to 3 months. Defrost in the fridge overnight. Reheat in a pan over a medium heat, adding a splash of water if needed.

 **TIPS** A great way to tempt kids to try this soup is by stirring in some cooked orzo or star-shaped pasta. It adds texture and makes the soup more filling!

To make your own vegetable stock, see page 136.

# VEGETABLE MINISTRINA

This soup is a family treasure, starting with Mattia's grandad and lovingly passed down to Nonna Laura (Mattia's mum) and then to us. I've added a little twist by including peas for some extra protein. It's our go-to remedy for those days when anyone's feeling under the weather.

    Serves: 2 adults and 2 children  Prep: 10 minutes Cook: 20 minutes  Age: from 6 months

NOTE: for babies under 1 year old, flatten the peas before serving

2 tablespoons extra virgin olive oil

¼ onion, diced

1 litre (34fl oz/4¼ cups) boiling water

1 low-salt vegetable stock cube

½ courgette, grated

1 small carrot, peeled and grated

80g (2¾oz/½ cup) frozen peas

4–5 cherry tomatoes, quartered

2–4 basil leaves

80–100g (2¾–3½oz) small pasta of your choice, such as stars or alphabet

grated Parmesan cheese, to serve (optional)

1. Heat the oil in a large saucepan over a medium heat, then add the onion and sauté for 2–3 minutes until translucent.

2. Add the boiling water, stock cube, courgette, carrot, peas, tomatoes and basil leaves, then bring to the boil and cook for 10 minutes.

3. Add the pasta and cook for 6–7 minutes, depending on the packet instructions, until al dente.

4. Remove from the heat and allow to cool slightly before serving.

5. Serve with Parmesan sprinkled on top, if desired. (Parmesan is optional but very much recommended!)

6. Buon appetito!

 **STORAGE** Store in an airtight container in the fridge for up to 2 days. Reheat over a low-medium heat, adding more broth or water as needed (the pasta will have absorbed the broth).

**TIPS** To make your own vegetable stock, see page 136.

# AVOCADO, CARROT AND COURGETTE MUFFINS

When we started weaning, this nutrient-rich recipe became a staple in our household. I would often prepare batches to freeze, ensuring it was always on hand for a nutritious snack, breakfast or a convenient on-the-go meal for my little ones.

 VEGETARIAN

 Makes: 9 muffins

 Prep: 10 minutes
Cook: 20 minutes

 Age: from 6 months (cut into quarters or strips for easy serving)

1 small ripe avocado, peeled, stoned and mashed

100g (3½oz) courgette, grated and squeezed to remove excess water

50g (1¾oz) carrot, peeled, grated and squeezed to remove excess water

3 medium eggs

50g (1¾oz/1¼ cups) grated Parmesan

150g (5½oz /1¼ cups) plain flour

2 teaspoons baking powder

unsalted butter or extra virgin olive oil, for greasing

1. Preheat the oven to 180°C/160°C fan/350°F/ gas 4 and grease a nine-hole muffin tin.

2. Combine all the ingredients in a large bowl and stir until a sticky, soft dough forms.

3. Spoon the mixture into the prepared tin.

4. Bake for 20–25 minutes until the muffins have risen and are golden on top, and a skewer inserted into the centre comes out clean.

5. Remove from the oven and allow to cool before serving.

6. Buon appetito!

 **STORAGE** Store in an airtight container in the fridge for up to 3 days, or freeze for up to 3 months. Defrost in the microwave for 1–2 minutes or overnight in the fridge. Reheat in the microwave for 30–60 seconds, or bake at 170°C/150°C fan/340°F/gas 3 for 10 minutes until hot.

**TIPS** For younger babies, consider making mini muffins for easier handling! Just remember to reduce the baking time by 10–15 minutes.

# CARROT AND LENTIL SOUP

Getting kids to eat enough vegetables can sometimes be tough. Soup is a great way to sneak in extra veggies without them even noticing. This soup includes lentils, too, adding vitamins, minerals, fibre and protein to one convenient bowl – perfect for picky eaters. Want to make it even more appealing? Add some small pasta.

    Serves: 2 adults and 2 children  Prep: 10 minutes Cook: 25 minutes  Age: from 6 months

30g (1oz) unsalted butter or dairy-free butter

80g (2¾oz) chopped onion

400g (14oz) carrots, peeled and chopped

180g (6¼oz) floury potatoes, peeled and chopped

100g (3½oz/½ cup) drained tinned green or brown lentils

500ml (17fl oz/2 cups) boiling water

1 low-salt vegetable stock cube

grated Parmesan cheese, to serve (optional)

1.  Heat the butter in a saucepan over a medium-high heat, then add the onion and sauté for 5–7 minutes until softened and golden.

2.  Add the carrots, potatoes, lentils, boiling water and stock cube. Stir well and bring to the boil, then reduce the heat, cover and simmer for 20–25 minutes, or until the vegetables are fork-tender.

3.  Remove from the heat and use a hand-held blender to purée the soup until smooth and creamy.

4.  Serve with grated Parmesan on top, if desired.

5.  Buon appetito!

 **STORAGE** Store in an airtight container in the fridge for up to 2 days, or freeze for up to 3 months in individual baby-sized servings. Thaw in the fridge overnight. Reheat over a low-medium heat, adding a splash of water if needed.

 **TIPS** Feel free to substitute the lentils for any beans depending on your preference or what you have in the cupboard.

To make your own vegetable stock, see page 136.

LUNCH AND DINNER

70

# HULK OMELETTE

This beloved recipe has been with me since the early days of weaning Grace, and it's still one of her favourites. Quick, simple and nutritious, it's my go-to lunch option.

   Serves: 1 child  Prep: 5 minutes Cook: 10 minutes  Age: from 6 months

**NOTE: don't add the peas for babies under 1 year old**

1 medium egg

15g (½oz) spinach leaves

1 tablespoon self-raising flour (see page 61 to make your own)

2 tablespoons grated Parmesan, Cheddar or dairy-free cheese

10g (½oz) frozen peas

extra virgin olive oil, for cooking

1. Put the egg and spinach into a food processor and pulse until smooth.

2. Add the flour and cheese and pulse again until smooth.

3. Heat a little olive oil in a frying pan over a low-medium heat, then pour in the egg mixture and top with the frozen peas.

4. Cover, then increase the heat to medium-high and cook for 3–4 minutes until bubbles form on top and the edges are dry. Flip and cook for a further 3–4 minutes until cooked through.

5. Allow to cool slightly, then cut into strips and serve.

6. Buon appetito!

 **STORAGE** Store in an airtight container in the fridge for up to 2 days, or freeze for up to 3 months. Defrost in the fridge overnight or gently reheat in a pan over low heat until warmed through.

 **TIPS** For a perfect result, use a frying pan no bigger than 12cm (5 inches) in diameter.

# EARTHY PASTA SOUP

I took a break from making soup for quite a while because I found it too messy to feed to my toddler. But this soup is a game-changer! Its chunky texture means I can give her plenty of pasta, peas and veggies with just a small amount of liquid, making it much easier for her to feed herself!

   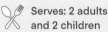 Serves: 2 adults and 2 children  Prep: 10 minutes Cook: 35 minutes  Age: from 6 months

**NOTE: blend the soup before adding the pasta for babies under 1 year old**

2 tablespoons extra virgin olive oil

1 onion, finely chopped

2 waxy potatoes, peeled and cut into small cubes

2 large carrots, peeled and cut into small cubes

140g (5oz/1 cup) frozen peas

1 litre (34fl oz/4¼ cups) boiling water

2 low-salt vegetable stock cubes

150g (5½oz) pasta of your choice

grated Parmesan cheese, to serve (optional)

1. Heat the olive oil in a large saucepan over a medium heat, add the onion and sauté for 5 minutes until soft.

2. Add the potatoes, carrots and peas and cook for about 5 minutes, stirring frequently.

3. Pour in the boiling water and add the stock cubes. Bring to the boil, then reduce the heat to low-medium and simmer for 15 minutes, covered but with a slight opening, stirring occasionally.

4. Add the pasta and cook according to the packet instructions until al dente.

5. Serve with grated Parmesan on top if desired.

6. Buon appetito!

 **STORAGE** Store in an airtight container in the fridge for up to 3 days, or freeze before adding the pasta for up to 3 months. Defrost in the fridge overnight. To reheat, warm in a saucepan over a medium heat, adding a splash of water if needed (and the pasta to cook through, if needed).

**TIPS** For this recipe, I like to use conchiglie-shaped pasta or ditalini/ditaloni.

To make your own vegetable stock, see page 136.

# PASTA E FAGIOLI

Pasta e fagioli (pasta and beans) always takes me back to my childhood; my grandma used to make it for me whenever we visited her! It always gives me the comforting and warm feeling of her home.

    Serves: 2 adults and 2 children  Prep: 10 minutes Cook: 30 minutes  Age: from 6 months

NOTE: for babies under 1 year old, blend the soup before adding the pasta

2 tablespoons extra virgin olive oil

1 onion, finely chopped

1 celery stick, chopped

1 large carrot, peeled and chopped

700ml (24fl oz/scant 3 cups) boiling water

300g (10½oz/1½ cups) cooked borlotti beans (drained tinned beans or cooked from dry)

1 tablespoon tomato purée

1 teaspoon sea salt (optional)

150g (5½oz) ditali or conchiglie pasta

grated Parmesan cheese, to serve (optional)

1. Heat the oil in a large saucepan over a medium heat and sauté the onion, celery and carrot for 3–4 minutes until soft.

2. Pour over the boiling water, then add the beans, tomato purée and salt, if using. Bring to the boil, then reduce the heat to low-medium, cover (leaving a slight opening) and simmer for 15 minutes, stirring occasionally.

3. Add the pasta and cook according to the packet instructions until al dente.

4. Serve with a sprinkle of Parmesan, if desired.

5. Buon appetito!

 **STORAGE** Store in an airtight container in the fridge for up to 3 days, or freeze before adding the pasta for up to 3 months. Defrost in the fridge overnight. To reheat, warm in a saucepan over a medium heat, adding a splash of water if needed (and the pasta to cook through, if needed).

**TIPS** Feel free to substitute the borlotti beans with any beans or chickpeas depending on your preference or what you have in the cupboard.

# LENTIL BALLS WITH TOMATO SAUCE

This recipe is a weekend favourite that the whole family enjoys. I especially love serving it with polenta, a classic side dish from the north of Italy, where I come from. Lentils are packed full of iron, an essential nutrient for babies and children.

    Serves: 1 adult and 2 children  Prep: 15 minutes Cook: 30 minutes  Age: from 6 months

**NOTE: for babies under 1 year old, cut each ball into four pieces before serving**

### FOR THE LENTIL BALLS

200g (7oz/1 cup) drained tinned brown lentils

30g (1oz) onion

3 tablespoons extra virgin olive oil

1 tablespoon tomato purée

40g (1½oz/½ cup) dried breadcrumbs, plus extra as needed

### FOR THE TOMATO SAUCE

3 tablespoons extra virgin olive oil

30g (1oz) onion, finely chopped

400g (14oz/1⅔ cups) passata

2 basil leaves

sea salt and freshly ground black pepper (optional)

### TO SERVE

polenta or mashed potatoes

1. Preheat the oven to 220°C/200°C fan/425°F/gas 7 and line a baking tray with baking paper.

2. First, make the lentil balls. Put the cooked lentils, onion, olive oil and tomato purée into a food processor and blend until smooth, scraping down the sides of the bowl as needed. Add the breadcrumbs and pulse again until the mixture is thick enough to create balls but not too sticky, adding more breadcrumbs if it is too sticky.

3. Shape the mixture into walnut-sized balls, then place on the prepared baking tray. Bake in the oven for 20 minutes until brown and crispy, turning the balls halfway through.

4. Meanwhile, make the tomato sauce. Heat the oil in a saucepan over a medium heat and sauté the onion for 5 minutes until soft and golden. Add the passata and whole basil leaves, then simmer for 15 minutes, stirring occasionally. Season with salt and pepper, if using.

5. Once cooked, allow the lentil balls to cool slightly, then transfer them to the tomato sauce and stir to coat.

6. Serve with polenta or mashed potatoes.

7. Buon appetito!

**STORAGE** Store in an airtight container in the fridge for up to 3 days, or freeze for up to 3 months. Defrost in the fridge overnight. Reheat in a saucepan over a medium heat until warmed through.

**TIPS** My go-to polenta is Polenta Valsugana – it only takes 5 minutes to cook! You can find it in most major supermarkets.

# CARROT AND PEA RISOTTO

This risotto was one of my favourites when I was little. The original recipe includes ham, but this version is meat-free.

  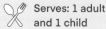 Serves: 1 adult and 1 child  Prep: 10 minutes / Cook: 20 minutes  Age: from 6 months

**NOTE: for babies under 1 year old, flatten the peas before serving**

2 tablespoons extra virgin olive oil

1 carrot, peeled and finely chopped

20g (¾oz) onion, finely chopped

160g (5¾oz/¾ cup) arborio rice

100g (3½oz/¾ cup) frozen peas

400ml (14fl oz/1⅔ cups) boiling water

1 low-salt vegetable stock cube

50g (1¾oz/½ cup) grated Parmesan cheese, plus extra to serve

1. Heat the oil in a saucepan over a medium heat, then add the carrot and onion and sauté for 3–4 minutes until starting to soften.

2. Add the rice, peas, boiling water and stock cube.

3. Reduce the heat to low-medium heat, cover and cook for 15–17 minutes until the rice is soft and the risotto is thick and creamy, stirring every few minutes to ensure it doesn't stick to the bottom of the pan and adding more boiling water if needed.

4. Remove the pan from the heat, stir in the Parmesan and allow to rest for 1–2 minutes.

5. Serve with more grated Parmesan, if desired.

6. Buon appetito!

**STORAGE** If cooled within 1 hour, it can be stored in an airtight container in the fridge for up to 3 days, or frozen for up to 3 months. Defrost overnight in the fridge. To reheat, add a little broth or water and gently warm over a low-medium heat, stirring often, until hot.

 **TIPS** To make your own vegetable stock, see page 136.

You could also make this recipe dairy-free by using a dairy-free cheese.

LUNCH AND DINNER

# LAZY PASTA

This is our go-to pasta dish to make every time we come back from a trip because it's made with ingredients we always have at home. With just a few simple ingredients, it's hard to believe this is one of Italy's most beloved pastas!

Serves: 1 adult and 1 child

Prep: 5 minutes
Cook: 10 minutes

Age: from 6 months

150g (5½oz) pasta of your choice

20g (¾oz) unsalted butter

30g (1oz/⅓ cup) grated Parmesan cheese, plus extra to serve

1. Bring a large saucepan of water to the boil and cook the pasta according to the packet instructions, then drain.

2. Melt the butter in a deep frying pan over a medium heat, making sure it does not burn.

3. Add the cooked pasta, then remove from the heat and add the Parmesan.

4. Serve with extra Parmesan sprinkled on top.

5. Buon appetito!

**STORAGE** I recommend enjoying this dish fresh. Leftovers, while convenient, just don't do justice to the creamy texture and flavour when reheated.

# COURGETTE PATTIES

Ricotta was my favourite cheese when I was little – it was always in our fridge, but I don't see it used much in the UK. I created these patties to share my love for ricotta with you. Enjoy making these for your family, like I do for mine.

Makes: 15 small patties     Prep: 10 minutes Cook: 20 minutes     Age: from 6 months

150g (5½oz) courgette, grated and squeezed to remove excess water

150g (5½oz) ricotta cheese

1 small egg

70g (2½oz/¾ cup) dried breadcrumbs, plus extra as needed

40g (1½oz/⅓ cup) grated Parmesan cheese

extra virgin olive oil, for drizzling

1. Preheat the oven to 200°C/180°C fan/400°F/ gas 6 and line a baking tray with baking paper.

2. Combine the courgette, ricotta, egg, breadcrumbs and Parmesan in a bowl and mix together until you have a thick consistency that can be shaped into patties – add more breadcrumbs if needed.

3. Shape the mixture into 14–15 small patties and place them on the prepared baking tray.

4. Drizzle a little olive oil over the patties, then bake for 20–25 minutes until golden and crispy, turning them halfway through.

5. Buon appetito!

 **STORAGE** Store in an airtight container in the fridge for up to 2 days, or freeze for up to 3 months. Defrost in the fridge overnight. Reheat in a frying pan over a medium heat until warmed through, or you can bake them in a low oven until heated through.

 **TIPS** Since courgettes contain a lot of water, it's crucial to thoroughly drain as much moisture as possible from them before making the patties.

You can also fry the patties: heat a little oil in a frying pan and cook the patties for about 2 minutes on each side until golden brown.

# CREAMY SALMON PASTA

*Mamma mia!* This pasta dish is incredibly tasty and super quick to make, taking only 15 minutes! Your whole family, from kids to adults, will love it!

    Serves: 2 adults and 2 children  Prep: 5 minutes / Cook: 15 minutes · Age: from 12 months

300g (10½oz) pasta of your choice

3 tablespoons extra virgin olive oil

30g (1oz) onion, finely chopped

150g (5½oz) smoked salmon, chopped

300ml (10½oz/1¼cups) double cream or dairy-free cream

fresh or dried parsley, for sprinkling

sea salt and freshly ground black pepper (optional)

1. Bring a large saucepan of salted water to the boil and cook the pasta according to the packet instructions, then drain, reserving some of the pasta water.

2. Meanwhile, heat the oil in a frying pan over a medium heat. Add the onion and cook for 5–7 minutes until softened.

3. Add the salmon and cook for a couple of minutes, then pour in the cream and 3 tablespoons of the pasta water. Cook over a gentle heat for 5 minutes.

4. Sprinkle over the parsley and black pepper, then stir in the drained pasta and mix well.

5. Buon appetito!

 **STORAGE** I recommend serving this dish fresh, as the creamy texture and flavour isn't quite as good when reheated.

 **TIPS** Smoked salmon is high in salt, so if you want to serve this to younger children (6 months and older), consider using cooked salmon fillet, which contains less salt.

LUNCH AND DINNER

# BROCCOLI PINWHEELS

If you haven't tried two-ingredient dough yet, you really need to jump on board! It's incredibly versatile and easy to make. I've made puff pastry broccoli pinwheels many times, but to be honest, I'm not a big fan of puff pastry. So, I finally figured out how to make them with this simple dough – and they turned out delicious!

    Makes: 10–12 pinwheels  Prep: 15 minutes Cook: 20 minutes  Age: from 9 months

3–4 broccoli florets

125g (4½oz/½ cup) Greek yoghurt or dairy-free Greek-style yoghurt

180g (6¼oz/1½ cups) self-raising flour (see page 61 to make your own), plus extra for dusting

20ml (1½ tablespoons) extra virgin olive oil or melted unsalted butter

80g (2¾oz/⅓ cup) cream cheese or dairy-free cream cheese

40g (1½oz/⅓ cup) grated Cheddar, Parmesan or dairy-free cheese

**TIPS** I use thick strained Greek yoghurt; if your yoghurt is not strained, you may find you need a little extra flour to get the right dough consistency.

1. Preheat the oven to 180°C/160°C fan/350°F/ gas 4 and line a baking tray with baking paper.

2. Steam or boil the broccoli florets for 2–3 minutes until soft, then chop finely and set aside.

3. Combine the yoghurt, flour and oil in a bowl. Mix together with your hands until a smooth dough forms.

4. Tip the dough out onto a lightly floured surface or a sheet of baking paper, then roll it out into a rectangle about 5mm (¼ inch) thick.

5. Spread the cream cheese evenly over the surface of the dough, leaving a 1cm (½ inch) border along one of the long edges.

6. Sprinkle the broccoli and grated cheese evenly over the cream cheese.

7. Starting from the long edge without the border, roll up the pastry. Brush a bit of water on the bare edge to help seal the roll. You should have a tight sausage shape.

8. Use a sharp knife to slice the roll into 1.5cm (½ inch) thick pinwheels.

9. Place the pinwheels on the prepared baking tray and bake in the oven for 15–20 minutes, checking occasionally to ensure they don't burn.

10. Remove from the oven and allow to cool slightly before serving.

11. Buon appetito!

Broccoli
Pinwheels

Sweet
Potato and
Courgette
Pizza
Pinwheels

**STORAGE** Store in an airtight container for up to 3 days or freeze for up to 1 month. To reheat, bake at 180°C/160°C fan/350°F/gas 4 for a few minutes until warmed through.

# SWEET POTATO AND COURGETTE PIZZA PINWHEELS

This is one of my favourite creations! These pinwheels are made from sweet potato, and hiding some courgettes inside makes them picky-eater proof.

   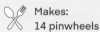 Makes: 14 pinwheels  Prep: 15 minutes Cook: 30 minutes  Age: from 9 months

300g (10½oz) sweet potato, peeled and roughly chopped

50g (1¾oz) courgette, grated and squeezed to remove excess water

250g (9oz/2 cups) self-raising flour (see page 61 to make your own), plus extra for dusting

100g (3½oz/⅓ cup) passata

⅓ teaspoon dried oregano

1–2 leaves basil, chopped

50–60g (1¾–2oz/½–⅔ cup) grated mozzarella, Cheddar or dairy-free cheese

 **TIPS** You may need a little more or less flour, depending on how much water you can squeeze out of the courgette. If the dough is too wet, add 1 tablespoon flour at a time until you reach the desired consistency. The dough should not be sticky but still soft.

1. Preheat the oven to 180°C/160°C fan/350°F/ gas 4 and line a baking tray with baking paper.

2. Steam the sweet potato over a gentle heat for 15–20 minutes until soft, then set aside. Once cooled, weigh out 250g (9oz) (any leftovers can be saved for later use).

3. Put the sweet potato into a large bowl and mash with a fork. Add the courgette and flour, then use your hands to bring the mixture together into a dough.

4. Tip the dough onto a floured surface, then roll it into a rectangle about 5mm (¼ inch) thick.

5. Combine the passata, oregano and basil in a small bowl, then spread it evenly over the dough, leaving a 1cm (½ inch) border along one of the long edges.

6. Sprinkle the cheese evenly over the tomato sauce.

7. Starting from the long edge without the border, roll up the pastry. Brush a bit of water on the bare edge to help seal the roll. You should have a tight sausage shape.

8. Use a sharp knife to slice the roll into 1.5cm (½ inch) thick pinwheels.

9. Place the pinwheels on the prepared baking tray and bake in the oven for 15–20 minutes, checking occasionally to ensure they don't burn.

10. Remove from the oven and allow to cool slightly before serving. Buon appetito!

# BROCCOLI AND CREAM CHEESE PATTIES

I promise you that with this recipe, you'll be able to get your kids to eat broccoli!

  VEGETARIAN DAIRY-FREE OPTION

 Makes: 14 patties

 Prep: 10 minutes
Cook: 15 minutes

 Age: from 6 months

180g (6¼oz) broccoli florets

100g (3½oz/½ cup) cream cheese or dairy-free cream cheese

40g (1½oz/⅓ cup) grated Parmesan cheese or dairy-free cheese

50g (1¾oz/⅔ cup) dried breadcrumbs, plus extra for coating

1 medium egg

pinch of sea salt (optional)

extra virgin olive oil, for cooking

1. Steam the broccoli florets for 5–6 minutes until soft. Remove from the heat and set aside cool.

2. Transfer the cooled florets to a large bowl and mash with a fork or finely chop with a knife.

3. Add the cream cheese, Parmesan, breadcrumbs, egg and salt, if using. Mix well until combined.

4. Shape the mixture into 14 walnut-sized balls, then slightly flatten with your hands and coat both sides with breadcrumbs.

5. Heat a glug of oil in a frying pan over a low-medium heat and fry the patties in batches for 2–3 minutes each side until golden and crisp.

6. Remove the patties from the pan and place on a kitchen paper to drain any excess oil.

7. Allow to cool slightly before serving.

8. Buon appetito!

**STORAGE** Store in an airtight container in the fridge for up to 3 days, or freeze for up to 2 months. Reheat the chilled patties in a pan or in the oven at 160°C/140°C fan/325°F/gas 2 for 10–15 minutes until crispy. Reheat from frozen at the same temperature for 15–20 minutes.

LUNCH AND DINNER

# VEGETABLE TOTS

I've never seen my girls enjoy vegetables more than they do when eating these tots. They are slightly crisp on the outside and soft and fluffy on the inside, making them perfect for baby-led weaning, too.

   Makes: 14 tots  Prep: 15 minutes / Cook: 35 minutes  Age: from 6 months

150g (5½oz) sweet potatoes, peeled and roughly chopped

100g (3½oz) carrots, peeled and roughly chopped

80g (2¾oz) broccoli or cauliflower florets

30g (1oz/⅓ cup) grated Cheddar cheese

20g (¾oz/¼ cup) grated Parmesan cheese (or more Cheddar)

30g (1oz/¼ cup) dried breadcrumbs

1. Preheat the oven to 200°C/180°C fan/400°F/ gas 6 and line a baking tray with baking paper.

2. Steam or boil the potatoes and carrots for 10 minutes, then add the broccoli or cauliflower florets and cook for a further 3–4 minutes, or until all the vegetables are soft. Drain well.

3. Transfer the vegetables to a large bowl and mash with a fork or a potato masher.

4. Add the cheeses and breadcrumbs, then stir together.

5. Scoop up a heaped tablespoon of the mixture and form it into a tot shape. Place on the prepared tray. Repeat with the remaining mixture.

6. Bake the tots in the oven for 20 minutes, or until golden.

7. Remove from the oven and allow to cool slightly before serving.

8. Buon appetito!

 **STORAGE** Store in an airtight container in the fridge for up to 2 days. Freeze on a baking tray until solid, then transfer to a freezer bag and store for up to 2 months. Reheat in the oven at 160°C/140°C fan/325°F/gas 2 until heated through and crispy on the outside.

 **TIPS** If your batter doesn't seem to be holding together well, add another tablespoon (or two) of breadcrumbs. Breadcrumbs works great in these tots, but if you prefer, you can replace it with the same weight of almond meal.

Vegetable
Tots

Broccoli and Cream
Cheese Patties

# SALMON FISHCAKES

These salmon fish cakes were Kate's favourite as a baby. They're practical, kid-friendly and delicious – a go-to for any parent looking to introduce fish in a tasty way. Salmon is a fantastic source of omega-3 fatty acids, specifically a type called DHA, which is essential for brain development and health in babies and children.

 Makes: 10 fishcakes   Prep: 10 minutes Cook: 35 minutes   Age: from 6 months

1 x 90g (3¼oz) salmon fillet

150g (5½oz) floury potatoes, peeled and chopped if large

50g (1¾oz/⅔ cup) dried breadcrumbs, plus extra as needed and for coating the fishcakes

30g (1oz/⅓ cup) grated Parmesan cheese

1 medium egg

⅓ teaspoon dried parsley

extra virgin olive oil, for frying

1. Steam the salmon and potatoes over a gentle heat for about 20 minutes, or until both are thoroughly cooked.

2. Remove the skin from the salmon and transfer it to a large bowl along with the potatoes. Use a fork or potato masher to mash them together. Stir in the breadcrumbs, grated Parmesan, egg and parsley until well combined. If the mixture is too moist, gradually add more breadcrumbs until it reaches a consistency that can be easily shaped.

3. Shape the mixture into 10 fishcakes, then coat each fishcake evenly with more breadcrumbs.

4. Heat a glug of oil in a frying pan over a medium-high heat, then fry the fishcakes for 2–3 minutes on each side until they are golden brown and crispy. Remove the fishcakes from the pan and place on kitchen paper to absorb any excess oil.

5. Allow the fishcakes to cool slightly before serving.

6. Buon appetito!

**STORAGE** Store the cooled fishcakes in an airtight container in the fridge for 1 day, or freeze for up to 2 months.

Defrost in the fridge overnight. Reheat in the oven at 180°C/160°C fan/350°F/gas 4 for 10–15 minutes until hot.

**TIPS** You can also bake the fishcakes in the oven. Don't coat them in breadcrumbs, but instead put them onto a baking tray lined with baking paper and drizzle lightly with olive oil. Bake at 180°C/160°C fan/350°F/gas 4 for 18–20 minutes until cooked through, turning them halfway through the baking time.

# CREAMY BROCCOLI PASTA

When my daughter Grace was starting out with baby-led weaning, one of her absolute favourites was this creamy broccoli pasta. Opt for protein-rich pasta varieties like lentil or pea pasta for an added nutritional boost.

    Serves: 2 children  Prep: 5 minutes Cook: 10 minutes  Age: from 6 months

100g (3½oz) pasta of your choice

8 broccoli florets

4 heaped tablespoons cream cheese or dairy-free cream cheese

sea salt and freshly ground black pepper (optional)

grated Parmesan cheese, to serve (optional)

1. Bring a large saucepan of water to the boil. Add the pasta and broccoli and cook according to the packet instructions. Drain, reserving some of the pasta water.

2. Put the cooked broccoli into a food processor along with the cream cheese and a couple of spoonfuls of pasta water. Season with salt and pepper, if using, then pulse until smooth and creamy. Add more water as needed to achieve your desired consistency.

3. Toss the cooked pasta with the broccoli sauce until well coated.

4. Serve with grated Parmesan on top, if desired.

5. Buon appetito!

 **STORAGE** Store in an airtight container in the fridge for up to 2 days. To reheat, warm gently over a low-medium heat, adding a splash of water to prevent it drying out.

 **TIPS** For young babies, you can use mascarpone instead of cream cheese as it's naturally lower in sodium.

LUNCH AND DINNER

# LENTIL BOLOGNESE

This is a family favourite that the girls ask for daily! It requires a bit of a time investment, but it's utterly rewarding and perfect for stocking up the freezer for those chaotic days. Packed with protein and fibre, it's not just satisfying but incredibly nourishing, too.

    Serves: 10–12 children   Prep: 15 minutes Cook: 45 minutes   Age: from 6 months

80ml (2¾fl oz/⅓ cup) extra virgin olive oil

60g (2oz) onion, finely chopped

60g (2oz) celery, finely chopped

60g (2oz) carrot, peeled and finely chopped

1 garlic clove, finely chopped

1½ tablespoons tomato purée

600ml (20fl oz/2½ cups) water, plus extra as needed

1 tablespoon white wine vinegar

1 tablespoon granulated sugar

200g (7oz/1 cup) dried brown or green lentils

700g (1lb 9oz/3 cups) passata

2 teaspoons sea salt (optional)

pasta of your choice, to serve

1. Heat the oil in a saucepan over a medium-high heat, then add the onion, celery, carrot and garlic and sauté for about 5 minutes until tender.

2. Add the tomato purée, 200ml (7fl oz/scant 1 cup) of the water, the vinegar, sugar, and lentils. Stir well, then cook for 8 minutes.

3. Stir in the passata, the remaining water and salt, if using.

4. Cover and bring to the boil, then reduce the heat to medium-low and simmer for 30–40 minutes, or until the lentils are tender and saucy, stirring occasionally. Gradually add more water if the sauce becomes too dry.

5. Serve with pasta.

6. Buon appetito!

 **STORAGE** Store in an airtight container in the fridge for up to 3 days, or freeze for up to 3 months. To defrost, simply place the frozen sauce in a saucepan and heat over a low-medium heat. Add a splash of water and stir occasionally until it's thawed and heated through. Alternatively, you can thaw the sauce in the fridge overnight. Once thawed, reheat gently as above.

 **TIPS** Using high-quality dried lentils is essential for achieving the best results with this recipe. I use lentil Bolognese for my homemade lasagne, too – find the recipe on page 124.

# PEA AND POTATO GNOCCHI

Homemade gnocchi has been one of my favourite foods since I was a child. These ones are not only delicious but also incredibly nutritious, as they're packed with peas and potatoes. While they're delightful with a simple tomato sauce, they truly shine with just butter and a sprinkle of Parmesan on top. *Buonissimi!*

Serves:
4 children

Prep: 25 minutes
Cook: 15 minutes

Age: from
9 months

NOTE: suitable from 9 months when cut lengthways into halves or quarters. For children around 2 years old, you can serve them whole

200g (7oz) floury potatoes (see Tip), peeled and cut into large pieces

200g (7oz/1¼ cups) frozen peas

200g (7oz/1⅔ cups) plain or wholemeal flour, plus extra as needed

**TO SERVE**
unsalted butter or dairy-free butter
grated Parmesan cheese (optional)

1. Steam the potatoes for 10–15 minutes until tender. Drain, mash until smooth, then set aside to cool.

2. Meanwhile, cook the peas in a small pan of boiling water for 4–5 minutes until tender. Drain, then transfer to a food processor and blend until they are smooth.

3. Add the puréed peas to the mashed potatoes and mix well.

4. Once cooled, add the flour and mix until the dough forms a ball. Add a little extra flour if the dough is too sticky.

5. On a lightly floured surface, roll portions of the dough into long sausage shapes, about 1.5cm (½ inch) thick.

6. Cut the dough into 1.5–2cm (½–1 inch) pieces to create the gnocchi.

7. Bring a large saucepan of salted water to a boil and drop in the gnocchi (you can do this in batches if needed). Cook for 2–3 minutes, or until the gnocchi rise to the top of the water.

8. Meanwhile, melt a knob of butter in a separate pan over a low heat. Remove from the heat. When the gnocchi are cooked, drain them and add to the pan with the melted butter, lightly tossing in the butter.

9. Serve with a generous sprinkle of Parmesan on top.

10. Buon appetito!

**STORAGE** Store the cooked gnocchi in an airtight container in the fridge for up to 2 days. To freeze uncooked gnocchi, arrange the gnocchi in a single layer on a baking sheet and freeze until solid, then transfer to a freezer bag or airtight container and freeze for up to 2 months. When ready to use, boil them directly from frozen as opposite, cooking them until they rise to the top of the water.

**TIP** Gradually add the flour until you achieve a soft but not sticky dough. Adding too much flour will make your gnocchi tough!

Yukon Gold potatoes are ideal for homemade gnocchi. They are dense, creamy and do not retain too much moisture.

# PASTA AL TONNO

Italy is divided in two when it comes to tuna pasta: there are those who add Parmesan cheese to it, and those who say fish and cheese should never be eaten together! Well, I belong to the first category – for me, it's a match made in heaven! Which side are you on? This tuna pasta is a simple and quick dish that I hope you'll love just as much as we do.

   Serves: 2–3 children  Prep: 5 minutes Cook: 20 minutes  Age: from 6 months

1 tablespoon extra virgin olive oil

30g (1oz) onion, finely chopped

1 garlic clove, peeled but left whole

1 x 145g (5oz) tin of tuna, drained

250g (9oz/1 cup) passata

160g (5¾oz) pasta of your choice

sea salt and freshly ground black pepper (optional)

1. Heat the oil in a large frying pan over a medium-high heat. Add the onion and garlic and sauté for 5–7 minutes until the onion has softened. Carefully remove the garlic.

2. Add the tuna and cook for a couple of minutes, then stir in the passata and season with salt and pepper if desired. Reduce the heat to low and cook for 10–15 minutes until it has reduced a little.

3. Meanwhile, bring a large saucepan of water to the boil and cook the pasta according to the packet instructions, then drain well.

4. Toss the drained pasta with the tuna sauce.

5. Buon appetito!

 **STORAGE** This is best enjoyed fresh, but leftovers can be stored in an airtight container in the fridge for up to 2 days. Reheat in the microwave or in a pan over a medium heat, adding a little extra water to thin the sauce if needed. The sauce can be made in advance and frozen in an airtight container or freezer bag for up to 2 months.

**TIPS** I recommend using tuna in olive oil for the best flavour. My favourite brand is Rio Mare.

For younger babies, use a pasta shape that is easy to grip, such as fusilli, and make sure it is well cooked.

# CANNELLINI BEAN NUGGETS

Looking to incorporate more beans into your child's diet but facing some hesitation? This recipe is an ideal pick! Its flavours and textures are sure to win them over. Don't be afraid of using herbs and spices in your children's food. They are a great way to add variety both for their tastebuds and gut-bugs!

     Makes: 15 nuggets   Prep: 10 minutes Cook: 10 minutes   Age: from 6 months

240g (8½oz) drained tinned cannellini beans

30g (1oz) onion, chopped

½ teaspoon dried rosemary

½ teaspoon dried parsley

40ml (1¼ fl oz) extra virgin olive oil, plus extra for frying

80g (2¾oz/1 cup) dried breadcrumbs, plus extra as needed and for coating

1. Combine the beans, onion, rosemary, parsley and oil in a food processor and blend until they are smooth.

2. Add the breadcrumbs and pulse until well combined. If the mixture is too sticky, add more breadcrumbs as needed.

3. Shape the mixture into 15 walnut-sized balls, then gently flatten to form nuggets. Coat each nugget in more breadcrumbs.

4. Heat a little oil in a frying pan over a medium heat and fry the nuggets in batches for 4–5 minutes on each side until golden and crispy, being careful when turning as they will be very soft.

5. Remove from the pan and place on kitchen paper to drain any excess oil.

6. Allow the nuggets to cool slightly and firm up before serving.

7. Buon appetito!

 **STORAGE** Store in an airtight container in the fridge for up to 2 days, or freeze for up to 3 months. Defrost in the fridge overnight. Reheat in a frying pan over a medium heat until warmed through or bake in the oven.

 **TIPS** You can also bake the nuggets in the oven. Place on a baking tray and drizzle with a little oil, then bake at 200°C/180°C fan/400°F/gas 6 for 18 minutes, turning halfway through.

# PASTINA AL POMODORO

A weekday dinner favourite: tomato pastina! It's a simple dish that, when prepared just right, tastes better than anything else. This recipe takes less than 20 minutes from start to finish and is made in just one pot, so you won't have much to wash up!

 VEGETARIAN  NO EGGS  Serves: 2 children  Prep: 5 minutes Cook: 15 minutes  Age: from 6 months

2 tablespoons extra virgin olive oil

30g (1oz) onion, finely chopped

120g (4¼oz/½ cup) passata

½ teaspoon sea salt (optional)

pinch of granulated sugar (optional)

2 basil leaves

150g (5½oz) orzo or small star-shaped pasta

350ml (12fl oz/1½ cups) boiling water, plus extra as needed

10g (½oz) unsalted butter

20g (¾oz/¼ cup) grated Parmesan cheese

1. Heat the oil in a saucepan over a medium heat, then add the onion and sauté for 5–7 minutes until softened and golden.

2. Add the passata, salt and sugar, if using, and basil leaves. Cook over a medium-low heat for 5 minutes.

3. Add the pasta and boiling water, then reduce the heat to low and simmer for 7–8 minutes until the pasta is al dente, stirring frequently to prevent sticking and adding more water if needed.

4. Remove from the heat and add the butter and Parmesan, then stir to combine.

5. Buon appetito!

 **STORAGE** Store in an airtight container in the fridge for up to 2 days, or freeze for up to 2 months. Defrost in the fridge overnight. Reheat over a low heat, adding a little water if needed to loosen.

 **TIPS** Adding a pinch of sugar is optional but recommended to balance the acidity of the tomato sauce.

LUNCH AND DINNER

# HOMEMADE PIZZA

In my Italian heart, I just knew I had to include a pizza recipe. Grace began her weaning journey with pizza, starting with the crust, and loved it from the very first day. She still does. It's become our special Friday evening treat, marking the start of the weekend. When I share pictures of this on Instagram, I always receive so many questions about the recipe. So, here we go!

  Makes: 1 large rectangular pizza (6–8 slices)  Prep: 6¼ hours  Cook: 25 minutes  Age: from 8 months

**FOR THE DOUGH**

280ml (9½fl oz/ 1¼ cups) room-temperature water

1 teaspoon fast-action dried yeast

500g (1lb 2oz/4 cups) strong white bread flour

30ml (1fl oz) extra virgin olive oil, plus extra for greasing

1 teaspoon sea salt

**FOR THE TOPPING**

250g (9oz/1 cup) passata

1 tablespoon extra virgin olive oil

3–4 basil leaves

1 teaspoon dried oregano

1–2 pinches of sea salt (optional)

1 x 125g (4½oz) ball of mozzarella, cut into small cubes

1. First, prepare the dough. Combine the water and yeast in a large bowl, then add the flour, oil and salt. Mix until they are combined.

2. Tip out the dough onto a clean surface and knead for about 5 minutes until it forms a smooth ball.

3. Lightly grease a large bowl with olive oil and place the dough inside. Cover with cling film and set aside to rise at room temperature for 6–8 hours, or until doubled in size.

4. When the dough has risen, preheat the oven to 230°C/ 210°C fan/450°F/gas 8 and grease a baking tray with olive oil.

5. Gently stretch the dough onto the baking tray, forming a rectangular shape or the shape of your tray. Continue stretching until it reaches your desired size.

6. Next, prepare the pizza sauce by combining the tomato, olive oil, basil, oregano and a pinch of salt, if using, in a bowl.

7. Spread the tomato sauce on the pizza base and bake in the oven for 15 minutes.

8. Remove the pizza from the oven and top with the mozzarella.

9. Return to the oven and bake for a further 10 minutes, or until the cheese is melted and golden.

10. Remove from the oven and allow to cool slightly before serving. Buon appetito!

**STORAGE** Store in the fridge for up to 2 days, or freeze for up to 3 months. Defrost in the fridge overnight. Reheat in a 180°C/160°C fan/350°F/gas 4 oven for 5 minutes or in the microwave until warmed through. To cook from frozen, bake at 180°C/160°C fan/350°F/gas 4 for 15–20 minutes or microwave on low until heated, checking to avoid overcooking.

**TIPS** I know it might seem like a long wait, but giving the pizza dough extra time to rise not only makes it easier on little tummies but also brings out a better taste. I promise you!

# CREAMY AVOCADO PASTA

I'm always looking for tasty ways to sneak in healthy fats and veggies that my kids will actually enjoy. Avocados are a nutrient-dense option for babies and children – not just one of their five-a-day, they also contribute all-important heart-healthy fats and gut-loving fibre. Since my daughters love avocado, I thought, why not try it in a pasta sauce?

    Serves: 2 children  Prep: 5 minutes Cook: 10 minutes  Age: from 6 months

100g (3½oz) pasta of your choice

1 ripe avocado, peeled and stoned

2 tablespoons ricotta cheese or dairy-free cream cheese

1 teaspoon extra virgin olive oil

1–2 tablespoons grated Parmesan cheese, plus extra to serve (optional)

1. Bring a large saucepan of water to the boil and cook the pasta according to the packet instructions, then drain, reserving some of the pasta water.

2. Meanwhile, mash the avocado with the ricotta and olive oil in a bowl. Add the Parmesan, if using, and a few tablespoons of the pasta water. Mix until smooth. Adjust the consistency by adding more water if needed.

3. Add the pasta to the avocado sauce and mix well until the pasta is coated.

4. Serve with grated Parmesan on top, if desired.

5. Buon appetito!

**STORAGE** This is best eaten fresh, but leftovers can be stored in the fridge for a few hours without much browning. To prevent browning, add a thin layer of olive oil on top.

# PASTA POMODORINI E MOZZARELLA

This dish is a family favourite – it's so simple yet so delicious. It is our go-to during the summer, especially when cherry tomatoes are in season. It's equally tasty served hot or cold and never disappoints. Did you know, when you heat tomatoes and combine them with a fat like olive oil, the antioxidant content actually increases!

   Serves: 1 adult and 1 child  Prep: 5 minutes Cook: 20 minutes  Age: from 6 months

NOTE: check page 8 for how to safely serve mozzarella to your baby

160–200g (5½–7oz) pasta of your choice

3 tablespoons extra virgin olive oil

1 garlic clove, finely chopped

250g (9oz/1½ cups) cherry or baby plum tomatoes, quartered

2–3 basil leaves

sea salt and freshly ground black pepper (optional)

**TO SERVE**

1 ball of mozzarella, cut into small pieces

grated Parmesan cheese

1. Bring a large saucepan of water to the boil and cook the pasta according to the packet instructions.

2. Meanwhile, heat the oil in a frying pan over medium-high heat, add the garlic and sauté for 5 minutes until golden.

3. Reduce the heat to low, then add the tomatoes, basil and salt and pepper, if using. Cover and cook for 10–15 minutes, stirring occasionally, until the tomatoes have softened but not completely broken down.

4. Remove the pan from the heat and add the cooked pasta, then stir well.

5. Serve with the mozzarella pieces on top and a sprinkle of Parmesan.

6. Buon appetito!

 **TIPS** Look for cherry or plum tomatoes, which are sweet and juicy and perfect for summer dishes. A mixture of yellow and red cherry tomatoes is the best choice!

# HOMEMADE PIADINA

I love making these homemade piadinas, especially in the summer when we want to enjoy warm evenings dining outdoors in the garden. I prepare the flatbreads and lay them out alongside a variety of fillings like cherry tomatoes, homemade pesto, sliced avocado and mozzarella, so everyone can create their own delicious combinations.

    Makes: 8 piadinas  Prep: 15 minutes Cook: 20 minutes  Age: from 12 months

NOTE: check page 8 for how to safely serve mozzarella to your baby

250g (9oz/1 cup) Greek yoghurt or dairy-free Greek-style yoghurt

200g (7oz/1²/₃ cups) self-raising flour (see page 61 to make your own), plus extra for dusting

150g (5½oz/1¼cups) wholemeal flour (or more self-raising flour for a lighter texture)

**TO SERVE**

sliced mozzarella

sliced cherry tomatoes

sliced avocado

homemade pesto

basil leaves

1. Combine the yoghurt and flours in a large bowl and mix until a smooth dough forms.

2. Tip out the dough onto a lightly floured surface, then divide it into eight equal-sized pieces and shape each one into a ball.

3. Re-flour the surface, if necessary, then roll out each dough ball into a thin circle.

4. Heat a dry frying pan over a medium-high heat. Cook the piadinas for 2–4 minutes on each side, or until golden brown with bubbles forming.

5. Once cooked, you can either fill the piadinas with your favourite ingredients while still warm in the pan or place them on the table along with the fillings and let everyone build their own perfect piadina.

6. Buon appetito!

 **STORAGE** Store in an airtight container for up to 7 days, or freeze for up to 4 months. Defrost at room temperature. Reheat in the oven at 180°C/160°C fan/350°F/gas 4 or in a pan until warmed through.

# COD BOCCONCINI

The recipe for these little cod bites comes from my mother-in-law. She makes them for the girls when we visit her in Italy, and even Grace, who isn't a fan of fish, loves them! They're very fluffy on the inside, and the fish taste isn't strong at all. Cod and other white fish are a rich source of iodine, an essential nutrient for children's growth and development. You can enjoy these bocconcini as a side dish or as a main with some veggies, potatoes and some sauce to dip them in.

   Makes: 20 bocconcini  Prep: 10 minutes Cook: 15 minutes  Age: from 6 months

60g (2oz/½ cup) plain flour

2 x 200–250g (7–9oz) skinless cod fillets, cut into squares

extra virgin olive oil, for frying

**TO SERVE**

lemon wedges

ketchup (optional)

1. Put the flour into a shallow bowl, then add the fish pieces and toss in the flour.

2. Heat a generous amount of olive oil in a frying pan over a medium-high heat.

3. Add the coated fish in batches and cook for 3–4 minutes on each side until brown.

4. Remove from the pan and place on kitchen paper to drain any excess oil.

5. Serve warm with the lemon wedges and ketchup, if desired.

6. Buon appetito!

 **STORAGE** I recommend eating these fresh, but if you have any leftovers, you can store them in an airtight container in the fridge for 1 day. Reheat in a pan or in the oven at 160°C/140°C fan/325°F/gas 2 until heated through.

 **TIPS** For even more flavour, add a sprinkle of dried parsley, black pepper or any other spice or herb to the flour.

# RISOTTO ALLA MILANESE

Another Italian classic: risotto alla Milanese! It's a famous dish from the city of Milan that is renowned for its beautiful golden colour – derived from saffron – and its irresistibly creamy and delicious taste. My grandma, Anna, used to lovingly prepare this special recipe for me when I was a child. I called it *risotto giallo* (yellow risotto)!

   Serves: 1 adult and 2 children    Prep: 10 minutes, plus 30 minutes infusing time
Cook: 20 minutes    Age: from 6 months

½ teaspoon saffron threads

3 tablespoons extra virgin olive oil

½ onion, finely chopped

160g (5¾oz/¾ cup) arborio rice

400ml (14fl oz/generous 1½ cups) boiling water

½ teaspoon sea salt (optional)

30g (1oz/⅓ cup) grated Parmesan cheese, plus extra to serve

20g (¾oz) unsalted butter

1. Place the saffron in a small glass and pour a little boiling water over it, ensuring it's completely covered, then set aside to infuse for 30–60 minutes.

2. Heat the olive oil in a saucepan over a medium heat, then add the onion and cook for 5–7 minutes until softened.

3. Add the rice, boiling water and salt, if using, then reduce the heat to low-medium, cover and cook for 10 minutes, stirring occasionally to prevent sticking.

4. After 10 minutes, add the saffron and its infused water, mix well, cover again and cook for a further 5 minutes until thick and creamy, adding a little more water if needed.

5. Remove from the heat and stir in the Parmesan and butter, then allow to rest for 1–2 minutes.

6. Serve with more Parmesan, if desired.

7. Buon appetito!

 **STORAGE** If the risotto is cooled within 1 hour, it can be frozen for up to 3 months. Defrost in the fridge overnight. Reheat in a pan over a medium heat until warmed through, adding a little water if necessary.

**TIPS** If your kids like peas, you could add some at the end of the rice cooking time to boost the protein content of the dish.

# AVOCADO COUSCOUS

Couscous is our favourite packed lunch for picnics in the park with friends.
It's easy to make, and even tastier when served cold.

    Serves: 1 adult and 1 child  Prep: 10 minutes Age: from 10 months

**NOTE: check page 8 for how to safely serve mozzarella to your baby**

120g (4¼oz/⅔ cup) couscous

240ml (8fl oz/1 cup) boiling water

1 ripe avocado, peeled, stoned and chopped

100g (3½oz/¾ cup) cherry tomatoes, quartered

125g (4½oz) mozzarella, cut into bite-sized pieces or shredded for younger babies

a drizzle of extra virgin olive oil

sea salt and freshly ground black pepper (optional)

1. Put the couscous into a bowl and pour over the boiling water. Cover immediately with a plate, then allow to steam for 5 minutes until tender and all the water has been absorbed.

2. Meanwhile, combine all the remaining ingredients in a bowl and mix well.

3. Once the couscous is ready, fluff it with a fork, then add to the bowl with other ingredients. Mix thoroughly.

4. Buon appetito!

 **STORAGE** This recipe is best enjoyed fresh, but it can be covered and stored in the fridge for up to 4 hours, though the avocado may darken during that time.

 **TIPS** Pour the boiling water evenly over the couscous to ensure even steaming. If the couscous isn't tender after steaming, add a splash or two more of boiling water, then cover and allow to steam for another minute.

For extra flavour, prepare the couscous with broth instead of water.

# LASAGNE

As an Italian, I couldn't leave homemade lasagne out of my book! In Italy, it's the dish of choice on Sundays. This mouthwatering delight hails from the Emilia-Romagna region, particularly from the city of Bologna (hence its name). When I make lasagne, I use my lentil Bolognese, but feel free to use your favourite ragù.

Serves: 8 adults and children

Prep: 25 minutes
Cook: 40 minutes

Age: from 9 months

700g (1lb 9oz/3 cups) Lentil Bolognese (see page 98) or ragù of your choice

150–200g (5½–7oz/1²⁄₃– 2 cups) grated Parmesan cheese

12 lasagne sheets

**FOR THE BESCIAMELLA**

1.25 litres (42fl oz/ 5½ cups) whole cow's milk or plant-based milk alternative

a pinch of sea salt (optional)

125g (4½oz) unsalted butter

125g (4½oz/1 cup) plain flour

1. Preheat the oven to 180°C/160°C fan/350°F/gas 4.

2. First, make the besciamella. Pour the milk into a saucepan and bring to a simmer over a high heat. Add the salt, if using, then remove from the heat and set aside.

3. Melt the butter in a separate saucepan over a low heat. Add the flour and whisk until smooth.

4. Pour in the milk while whisking vigorously to avoid any lumps forming. Keep whisking for 10–15 minutes until you have a fairly thick consistency.

5. Now, assemble the lasagne. Spread about 2–3 tablespoons of the Bolognese and a few spoonfuls of besciamella over the bottom of a 31 x 21cm (12¼ x 8¼ inch) baking dish. Place a layer of lasagne sheets on top, then pour over a quarter of the besciamella, a quarter of the Bolognese sauce and a quarter of the Parmesan cheese. Repeat the layers of pasta and sauces until you have four layers. Finish with a layer of besciamella and Bolognese sauce, ensuring no pasta is poking through, then scatter over the remaining Parmesan.

6. Bake in the oven for 40 minutes until golden and bubbling.

7. Remove from the oven and allow the lasagne to stand for 10 minutes before serving.

8. Buon appetito!

# TUNA BALLS

This recipe was taught to me by my mother-in-law, Laura. She always makes these when we visit her in Italy, and the girls go crazy for them – seriously, they vanish even before we all sit down at the table! So, I decided to include the recipe in the book, hoping that your kids will enjoy them just as much.

 Makes:
16 small balls

 Prep: 10 minutes
Cook: 10 minutes

 Age: from
6 months

1 x 145g (5½oz) tin of tuna, drained

125g (4½oz/½ cup) ricotta cheese

60g (2oz/¾ cup) dried breadcrumbs, plus extra for coating

1 medium egg

½ teaspoon dried or finely chopped fresh parsley

extra virgin olive oil, for frying

1. Flake the tuna into a bowl, then add the ricotta and mix well.

2. Add the breadcrumbs, egg and parsley, and mix together with a fork until completely combined.

3. Roll the mixture into 16 walnut-sized balls, then coat the balls in more breadcrumbs.

4. Heat a little olive oil in a frying pan over medium-high heat and fry the balls in batches for about 5 minutes until golden and crisp.

5. Remove from the pan and place on kitchen paper to drain any excess oil.

6. Buon appetito!

 **STORAGE** Store in the fridge in an airtight container for up to 2 days, or freeze for up to 3 months. Defrost in the fridge overnight. Reheat in a frying pan over a medium heat until warmed through, or bake in a low oven until heated through.

**TIPS** You can also bake the balls in the oven at 200°C/180°C fan/400°F/gas 6 for about 15 minutes, but they will not look as good as the fried ones.

You can substitute the tuna with tinned salmon if you prefer. For babies under 1 year old, you can shape them into finger shapes, which are easier to hold.

LUNCH AND DINNER

# GREEN RISOTTO

Whenever I ask Grace what she wants to eat, her answer is always 'the green risotto'! This dish is packed with iron and all the nutrients your little one needs to keep growing strong.

   Serves: 2 children  Prep: 5 minutes Cook: 25 minutes  Age: from 6 months

**NOTE: for babies under 1 year old, flatten the peas before serving**

2 tablespoons extra virgin olive oil

30g (1oz) onion, finely chopped

50g (1¾oz) spinach leaves

500ml (17fl oz/2 cups) water, plus extra as needed

160g (5¾oz/¾ cup) arborio rice

1 low-salt vegetable stock cube

60g (2oz/⅓ cup) frozen peas

30g (1oz/⅓ cup) grated Parmesan cheese, plus extra to serve

10g (½oz) unsalted butter

1. Heat the oil in a saucepan over a medium heat, then add the onion and sauté for 5–7 minutes until softened.

2. Meanwhile, put the spinach and water into a food processor and blend until smooth, then add to the pan.

3. Add the rice and stock cube, bring to the boil, reduce the heat to low-medium and cook for 10 minutes, stirring every few minutes to prevent sticking.

4. Add the peas and cook for another 7 minutes, adding a bit more water if needed.

5. Once the rice is cooked and the risotto is thick and creamy, remove from the heat. Stir in the grated Parmesan and the butter and allow to rest for 1–2 minutes.

6. Serve with an extra sprinkle of grated Parmesan, if desired.

7. Buon appetito!

 **STORAGE** If cooled within 1 hour, the risotto can be stored in an airtight container in the fridge for up to 2 days, or frozen for up to 3 months. Defrost in the fridge overnight. Reheat over a medium heat until heated through.

LUNCH AND DINNER

**TIPS** This green risotto is so hearty and packed with veggies that it makes for a satisfying dinner on its own, but for an extra boost of nutrition, I usually serve it with a side of fresh fruit.

For older children and adults, you can add 1 teaspoon salt if using an unsalted stock.

To make your own vegetable stock, see page 136.

# COURGETTE CARROT FRITTATA FINGERS

This recipe is for my daughter, Kate, who always answers 'frittata' when asked what she wants for lunch or dinner! I love frittatas because they require minimal effort and create little mess, and they're ready in under half an hour. Perfect for freezing to whip out on busy days or for packing for picnics and lunch boxes, especially when shaped into fingers.

 VEGETARIAN

 Makes: 12 frittata fingers

 Prep: 10 minutes
Cook: 20 minutes

 Age: from 6 months

100g (3½oz) courgette, grated and squeezed to remove excess water

50g (1¾oz/½ cup) carrot, peeled, grated and squeezed to remove excess water

3 large eggs, beaten

60 (2oz/⅔ cup) grated Cheddar cheese

3–4 cherry tomatoes, sliced

grated Parmesan cheese, for sprinkling (optional)

1. Preheat the oven to 180°C/160°C fan/350°F/ gas 4 and line a 21 x 21cm (8¼ x 8¼ inch) baking dish with baking paper.

2. Combine the courgette, carrot, eggs and Cheddar in a bowl and mix well.

3. Transfer the mixture to the prepared baking dish and top with the cherry tomatoes, then sprinkle with Parmesan, if using.

4. Bake in the oven for 20–25 minutes, or until golden on top.

5. Remove from the oven, cut into fingers and serve.

6. Buon appetito!

 **STORAGE** Store in an airtight container in the fridge for up to 2 days, or freeze for up to 2 months. Defrost in the fridge overnight. Reheat in the oven at 160°C/140°C fan/325°F/gas 2 for 5–10 minutes until heated through or warm in the microwave.

Broccoli Salmon
Frittata Fingers

Courgette Carrot
Frittata Fingers

# BROCCOLI SALMON FRITTATA FINGERS

Thanks to the salmon, this frittata is loaded with omega-3 fatty acids and packed with protein. It's not only a delicious choice for breakfast, brunch or lunch, but also a fantastic way to use up leftover cooked salmon and broccoli.

 Makes: 12 frittata fingers

 Prep: 10 minutes
Cook: 40 minutes

 Age: from 6 months

100g (3½oz) broccoli florets

1 x 90g (3¼oz) salmon fillet

3 large eggs

30g (1oz/⅓ cup) grated Cheddar or Parmesan cheese

1. Steam the broccoli and salmon over a gentle heat for about 20 minutes or until thoroughly cooked.

2. Preheat the oven to 200°C/180°C fan/400°F/ gas 6 and line a 21 x 21cm (8¼ x 8¼ inch) baking dish with baking paper.

3. Remove the skin from the salmon, then place in a bowl along with the broccoli and mash together with a fork.

4. Add the eggs and cheese and mix well.

5. Transfer the mixture to the prepared baking dish, then bake the frittata in the oven for 20–25 minutes, or until golden on top.

6. Cut into fingers and serve.

7. Buon appetito!

 **STORAGE** Store in an airtight container in the fridge for up to 2 days, or freeze for up to 2 months. Defrost in the fridge overnight. Reheat in the oven at 160°C/140°C fan/325°F/gas 2 for 20–25 minutes until heated through.

LUNCH AND DINNER

# VEGGIE PASTA SAUCE

When I'm feeling lazy but still want to serve my family something nutritious, I turn to this pasta sauce. It's incredibly easy: all you have to do is blend all the veggies, transfer them to a saucepan and then simmer with the passata. So simple!

    Serves: 6 children  Prep: 5 minutes Cook: 30 minutes  Age: from 6 months

30g (1oz) onion, roughly chopped

60g (2oz) carrot, peeled and roughly chopped

60g (2oz) celery, roughly chopped

1 garlic clove

4 basil leaves

4 tablespoons extra virgin olive oil

400g (14oz/1²⁄₃ cups) passata

1 teaspoon sea salt (optional)

**TO SERVE**

pasta of your choice

grated Parmesan cheese (optional)

1. Put the onion, carrot, celery, garlic and basil into a food processor and pulse until finely chopped (or very finely chopped/puréed for younger babies).

2. Transfer to a saucepan, add the olive oil, and sauté for 6–8 minutes until starting to soften.

3. Add the passata and salt, if using. Bring to the boil, then reduce the heat and cook, covered, for about 20 minutes until the vegetables are soft.

4. Serve with your favourite pasta, topped with grated Parmesan, or allow it to fully cool before freezing for the busiest days!

5. Buon appetito!

 **STORAGE** Store in an airtight container in the fridge for up to 3 days, or freeze for up to 3 months in individual baby-sized servings. To defrost, simply place the frozen sauce in a saucepan and heat over a low-medium heat. Add a splash of water and stir occasionally until it's thawed and heated through. Alternatively, you can thaw the sauce in the fridge overnight. Once thawed, reheat gently as above.

 **TIPS** Got a picky eater who's not keen on veggie chunks? No problema! Just blend the sauce before mixing it with the pasta.

# PESTO ALLA GENOVESE

Pesto alla Genovese has recently made a comeback in my house, thanks to my best friend, Marika. She is from Genoa, the city known for pesto in the Liguria region of Italy. I love using homemade pesto to add flavour to tomato pasta sauces and sandwiches, too.

   Serves: 2 adults and 2 children    Prep: 5 minutes     Age: from 6 months

30g (1oz) Parmesan cheese, cut into pieces

30g (1oz) basil leaves

25g (1oz) pine nuts

50ml (1¾fl oz) extra virgin olive oil

pinch of salt (optional)

1. Put the Parmesan into a food processor and pulse until fine.

2. Add the rest of the ingredients and pulse several times until well combined.

 **STORAGE** Store in an airtight container in the fridge for 5 days, or freeze for up to 3 months. To freeze, pour into an ice-cube tray and freeze, then remove the cubes from the tray and transfer them to a freezer bag. Add the frozen cubes directly to your hot food or let them defrost at room temperature.

 **TIPS** If you want to always have pesto in your freezer, just double the recipe and you'll have more to freeze.

# KID-FRIENDLY VEGETABLE STOCK CUBES

When my little ones were just babies, I learned how to make homemade vegetable stock cubes, a delicious addition to meals without any added salt or artificial additives. And guess what? It's so effortless that I still make them regularly. Plus, it's a fantastic way to make use of those leftover veggies hiding in the fridge!

    Makes: 15 stock cubes  Prep: 5 minutes Cook: 30 minutes  Age: from 6 months

1 tablespoon extra virgin olive oil

250g (9oz) carrots, peeled and diced

120g (4¼oz) onions, diced

100g (3½oz) potato, peeled and diced

200g (7oz) celery, diced

50g (1¾oz) small tomatoes, halved

100g (3½oz) courgette, diced

1 garlic clove

6 basil leaves

6 parsley leaves

1. Heat the oil in a large saucepan over a medium heat, then add the chopped vegetables and whole garlic clove and sauté for a few minutes. Simmer until the liquid from the vegetables has evaporated and the veggies are soft, stirring frequently.

2. Add the basil and parsley, then pour everything into a food processor and blend until smooth.

3. Pour the mixture back into the pan and cook for a further 5 minutes, stirring constantly.

4. Pour the mixture onto a piece of parchment paper and shape it into a block using a spatula. Place the block in the freezer for 12 hours until fully frozen.

5. Once frozen, cut the block into cubes. You should get about 15 cubes.

6. Store the vegetable cubes in a freezer bag, separating them with parchment paper squares to prevent sticking.

 **STORAGE** Freeze for up to 4 months.

 **TIPS** Keep in mind that these stock cubes don't contain any salt – it's all about adding flavour to your dishes. When it comes to salt, you're in charge of adding it to your taste.

You can also freeze the mixture in an ice-cube tray.

# SNACKS

# SWEET POTATO BISCUITS

The perfect on-the-go snack – a favourite of both my little ones and myself! Made with simple ingredients you likely already have at home, I've added wholemeal flour for extra fibre, but regular flour works just as well. One bite and you won't be able to stop!

    Makes: 40 biscuits  Prep: 15 minutes Cook: 25 minutes  Age: from 6 months

230g (8¼oz) sweet potato, peeled and roughly chopped

50g (1¾oz) unsalted butter or dairy-free butter, melted

150g (5½oz/1¼ cups) self-raising flour (see page 61 to make your own)

30g (1oz/¼ cup) wholemeal flour (or more self-raising flour)

1. Preheat the oven to 180°C/160°C fan/350°F/gas 4.

2. Steam the sweet potato over a gentle heat for 15–20 minutes until soft, then set aside to cool. Once cooled, weigh out 200g (7oz) of the potato (any leftovers can be discarded or saved for later use).

3. Put the sweet potato into a large bowl and mash with a fork.

4. Add the melted butter and flours and mix together to form a dough.

5. Put the dough onto a sheet of baking paper and roll out to 5mm (¼ inch) thick, then cut into shapes with a cookie cutter. Alternatively, you can cut it with a sharp knife or a pizza wheel to make small squares.

6. Transfer the baking paper and biscuits to a baking tray and bake for 10 minutes until lightly golden, checking to make sure they don't overcook.

7. Remove from the oven and allow to cool before serving.

8. Buon appetito!

 **STORAGE** Store in an airtight container for 3 days, or freeze for up to 3 months. Defrost in the fridge overnight or at room temperature for a few hours.

# BANANA BREAD MUFFINS

These banana bread muffins are sweetened with bananas only, making them perfect for babies of any age! For best results and a naturally sweet flavour, choose fully ripe bananas for this recipe!

    Makes: 6 muffins  Prep: 10 minutes Cook: 20 minutes  Age: from 6 months

**NOTE: don't add the chocolate for children under 2 years old**

200g (7oz) overripe bananas

100g (3½oz/¾ cup) oat flour (to make your own, see page 52)

15g (½oz) smooth peanut butter

2 teaspoons baking powder

30ml (1fl oz) whole cow's milk or plant-based milk alternative

30g (1oz) dark chocolate, chopped (optional)

1. Preheat the oven to 180°C/160°C fan/350°F/gas 4 and line a six-hole muffin tin with muffin liners.

2. In a bowl, mash the bananas, then add the remaining ingredients and mix well.

3. Spoon the mixture into the muffin liners and bake for 18–20 minutes until golden and a skewer inserted into the centre comes out clean.

4. Remove from the oven and allow to cool before serving.

5. Buon appetito!

**STORAGE** Store in an airtight container for up to 3 days, or freeze for up to 3 months. Defrost in the fridge overnight.

You can warm the muffins up in a low oven before serving if desired.

Banana Spinach
Muffins

Banana
Bread Muffins

# BANANA SPINACH MUFFINS

You all know my love for sneaking veggies into baking, right? Well, get ready for these blender banana and spinach muffins – they're packed with fruits and vegetables and make the perfect grab-and-go breakfast or snack.

    Makes: 6 muffins  Prep: 10 minutes Cook : 20 minutes  Age: from 6 months

NOTE: don't add the chocolate for children under 2 years old

200g (7oz) overripe bananas

30g (1oz) baby spinach leaves

1 tablespoon smooth peanut butter

1½ teaspoons baking powder

40ml (1¼ fl oz) whole cow's milk or plant-based milk alternative

125g (4½oz/1 cup) wholemeal or plain flour

30g (1oz/¼ cup) chopped dark chocolate (optional)

1. Preheat the oven to 180°C/160°C fan/350°F/ gas 4 and line a six-hole muffin tin with muffin liners.

2. Put all the ingredients except the flour and chocolate, if using, into a food processor. Blend until very smooth.

3. Add the flour and pulse again until well combined.

4. Stir in the chocolate and mix gently.

5. Spoon the mixture into the muffin liners, then bake in the oven for 18–20 minutes until lightly browned around the edges and a skewer inserted into the centres comes out clean.

6. Remove from the oven and allow to cool before serving.

7. Buon appetito!

 **STORAGE** Store in an airtight container for up to 3 days, or freeze for up to 3 months. Defrost in the fridge overnight.

Warm in the oven at 160°C/140°C fan/325°F/gas 2 before serving, if desired.

 **TIPS** As this recipe is sweetened by the bananas only, try to use very ripe bananas with brown spots for the best natural sweetness.

SNACKS

# SWEET POTATO MUFFINS

These muffins are great for kids of all ages and make a great after-school snack or lunchbox filler. The glorious orange flesh of sweet potatoes is a great source of plant-based Vitamin A – a key nutrient for eye health in babies and children.

   Makes: 6 muffins 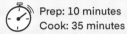 Prep: 10 minutes Cook: 35 minutes  Age: from 6 months

**NOTE: don't add the chocolate for children under 2 years old**

120g (4¼oz) sweet potato, peeled and chopped

1 medium egg

30g (1oz/scant ¼ cup) coconut sugar (optional)

20g (¾oz) unsalted butter or dairy-free butter, melted, plus extra for greasing

60ml (2floz/¼ cup) whole cow's milk or plant-based milk alternative

60g (2oz/½ cup) wholemeal or plain flour

30g (1oz/¼ cup) oat flour (to make your own, see page 52)

1½ teaspoons baking powder

a pinch of ground cinnamon (optional)

20g (¾oz) dark chocolate, chopped (optional)

1. Preheat the oven to 180°C/160°C fan/350°F/gas 4 and line a six-hole muffin tin with muffin liners or grease with butter or oil.

2. Steam the sweet potato over a gentle heat for 15–20 minutes until soft, then set aside to cool. Once cooled, weigh out 100g (3½oz) of the potato (any leftovers can be discarded or saved for later use).

3. Combine the sweet potato, egg and coconut sugar, if using, melted butter and milk in a large bowl and mix until well combined.

4. In a separate bowl, whisk together the flour, oat flour, baking powder and cinnamon, if using.

5. Gradually add the dry ingredients to the wet ingredients, stirring until just combined to avoid overmixing. Fold in most of the chocolate, if using, reserving some for the top.

6. Divide the mixture evenly into the muffin liners, filling each about three quarters full. Sprinkle the reserved chocolate on top.

7. Bake in the oven for 18–20 minutes, or until a skewer inserted into the centre comes out clean.

8. Remove from the oven and allow to cool slightly before serving. Buon appetito!

**STORAGE** Store in an airtight container for up to 3 days, or freeze for up to 3 months. Defrost in the fridge overnight. Warm in the oven at 160°C/140°C fan/325°F/gas 2 before serving, if desired.

# GREEN EGG MUFFINS

Quick and nutritious egg muffins packed with iron and protein – perfect for any time of day! Make them ahead and stash them in the fridge until you need them.

Makes: 6 muffins

Prep: 10 minutes
Cook: 25 minutes

Age: from 6 months

60g (2oz) broccoli florets

10g (½oz) baby spinach leaves

3 large eggs

40g (1½oz/⅓ cup) grated Cheddar or dairy-free cheese (optional)

extra virgin olive oil or unsalted butter, for greasing (optional)

1. Preheat the oven to 180°C/160°C fan/350°F/ gas 4 and line a six-hole muffin tin with muffin liners or grease the holes with olive oil or butter.

2. Steam or boil the broccoli florets for about 5 minutes or until tender, then drain, chop and set aside in a bowl.

3. Put the spinach and eggs into a food processor and pulse until combined.

4. Add the egg mixture to the broccoli along with the cheese and mix well.

5. Spoon the mixture into the muffin liners, then bake in the oven for 20–25 minutes, or until the muffins are golden on top.

6. Remove from the oven and allow to cool slightly before serving.

7. Buon appetito!

 **STORAGE** Store in an airtight container in the fridge for up to 3 days, or freeze for up to 3 months. Defrost in the fridge overnight. Reheat in the oven at 160°C/140°C fan/325°F/gas 2 for 5–10 minutes until heated through.

 **TIPS** You can use Cheddar cheese, mozzarella, feta cheese (for older children, due to salt content), Parmesan or another type of shredded cheese you like. To make dairy-free, swap the cheese for a dairy-free variety, or omit it altogether.

Be sure to use silicone muffin liners or grease your muffin tin really well to avoid sticking.

SNACKS

# CHOC CHIP COOKIES

My kids love chocolate chip cookies for an afternoon snack, so I set out to find the healthiest version. And voilà! These cookies are rich in fibre thanks to the wholemeal flour and ground almonds, and have just a touch of sugar. Plus, they're egg-free, so they're perfect for those little ones with allergies. Did I mention how incredibly delicious they are?

    Makes: 10 cookies  Prep: 10 minutes Cook: 10 minutes  Age: from 2 years

100g (3½oz/⅔ cup) wholemeal flour

50g (1¾oz/½ cup) ground almonds

50g (1¾oz/¼ cup) coconut sugar

1 teaspoon baking powder

20ml (4 teaspoons) whole cow's milk or plant-based milk alternative

60ml (2fl oz/¼ cup) melted coconut oil or unsalted butter

20–30g (¾–1oz) chopped dark chocolate

1. Preheat the oven to 180°C/160°C fan/ 350°F/gas 4 and line a baking sheet with baking paper.

2. Combine the flour, ground almonds, sugar and baking powder in a large bowl.

3. Add the melted coconut oil or butter and milk to the dry ingredients. Mix until well combined, then fold in the chocolate.

4. Divide the mixture into 10 equal-sized balls. Place the balls on the prepared baking sheet and gently press down to create a cookie shape.

5. Bake in the oven for 10–12 minutes, or until the edges are golden brown.

6. Remove from the oven and allow to cool completely before serving – they will set while cooling.

7. Buon appetito!

 **STORAGE** Store in an airtight container for up to 4 days. Freeze in a single layer on a baking sheet, then transfer to a freezer bag and freeze for up to 2 months. Defrost at room temperature for 30 minutes or warm in the oven at 150°C/130°C fan/300°F/gas 2 for 5–10 minutes.

 **TIPS** When choosing dark chocolate, go for one with high cocoa (70 per cent or higher), with minimal ingredients, low sugar and no additives.

# APPLE BANANA COOKIES

When I see an overripe banana, the first recipe that comes to mind is these cookies. They're simple, require just a handful of ingredients that I always have at home, and take just a few minutes to make.

    Makes: 9 cookies 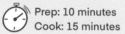 Prep: 10 minutes Cook: 15 minutes  Age: from 6 months

**NOTE: don't add the chocolate for children under 2 years old**

100g (3½oz) overripe banana

60g (2oz) apple, peeled and grated

1 tablespoon smooth peanut butter (or any nut or seed butter)

100g (3½oz/1 cup) porridge oats

20g (¾oz) dark chocolate, chopped (optional)

1. Preheat the oven to 180°C/160°C fan/ 350°F/gas 4 and line a baking tray with baking paper.

2. Mash the banana in a bowl, then add the grated apple and peanut butter and mix until combined.

3. Add the oats and chocolate, if using, and mix well again.

4. Roll into balls, then place on the prepared baking tray.

5. Slightly press down on each ball with your hand to form the cookies.

6. Bake in the oven for 15 minutes until the cookies are lightly browned and set.

7. Remove from the oven and allow to cool before serving.

8. Buon appetito!

 **STORAGE** Store in an airtight container for 3 days, or freeze for up to 3 months. Defrost overnight in the fridge, or at room temperature for a few hours.

 **TIPS** Use overripe bananas with plenty of brown spots for maximum sweetness, as these cookies obtain their sweetness from the banana only.

Apple Carrot
Biscuits

Apple Banana
Cookies

# APPLE CARROT BISCUITS

I've lost count of all the versions of these biscuits I've come up with! These ones are made with carrot and apple, and let me tell you, once you take a bite, you won't be able to stop. Taste to believe!

    Makes: 40–50 mini biscuits  Prep: 10 minutes Cook: 25 minutes  Age: from 6 months

150g (5½oz) crisp eating apple, peeled and roughly chopped

140g (5oz) carrots, peeled and roughly chopped

30g (1oz) unsalted butter or dairy-free butter, melted

170g (6oz/1⅓ cups) self-raising flour (see page 61 to make your own), plus extra as needed

40g (1½oz/⅓ cup) wholemeal flour (or more self-raising flour)

1. Preheat the oven to 180°C/160°C fan/350°F/gas 4.

2. Steam the apples and carrots over a gentle heat for 15–20 minutes until soft, then set aside to cool. Once cooled, weigh out 100g (3½oz) of the apple and 120g (4¼oz) of the carrots (any leftovers can be discarded or saved for later use).

3. Put the cooked carrots and apple into a large bowl and mash with a fork or potato masher.

4. Add the melted butter and flours and mix together to form a dough, adding a little more flour if the dough is too sticky.

5. Put the dough onto a sheet of baking paper and roll out to 5mm (¼ inch) thick, then cut into shapes with a cookie cutter. Alternatively, you can cut it with a sharp knife or a pizza wheel to make small squares.

6. Transfer the baking paper and biscuits to a baking tray and bake in the oven for 10 minutes until lightly golden, checking to make sure they don't overcook.

7. Remove from the oven and allow the biscuits to cool before serving.

8. Buon appetito!

 **STORAGE** Store in an airtight container for 3 days, or freeze for up to 3 months. Defrost in the fridge overnight or at room temperature for a few hours.

 **TIPS** For babies under 1 year old, shape the biscuits into finger-length strips for easier handling.

SNACKS

# HOMEMADE HUMMUS

I love serving hummus to the girls because it's rich in iron and pairs well with practically anything. Shop-bought hummus may not be ideal for young babies due to its high salt levels, but don't worry! Making your own is super easy and tastes delicious, even without salt. Plus, you can always set aside a portion for grown-ups to season to taste. We love spreading hummus on toast or using it as a dip for soft, cooked vegetables or fresh cucumber sticks. Tahini is also a great source of plant-based calcium and healthy fats.

     Serves: 2 adults and 2 children   Prep: 5 minutes   Age: from 6 months

200g (7oz/1 cup) tinned chickpeas, drained

1 tablespoon tahini

juice of ½ lemon

3 tablespoons extra virgin olive oil

2–2½ tablespoons water

pinch of sea salt (optional)

1. Combine all the ingredients in a food processor and blend until smooth and creamy, adding more water as needed.

2. Buon appetito!

**STORAGE**  Store in an airtight container in the fridge for up to 1 week, or freeze, covered with a thin layer of olive oil, for up to 1 month. Defrost in the fridge overnight.

# CHEESE AND OLIVE BREADSTICKS

This was the very first recipe I created for this book, and it remains a cherished favourite. These breadsticks require no rising time and are wonderfully versatile – they're ideal as a snack on their own or as a delightful accompaniment to soups.

   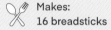 Makes: 16 breadsticks —  Prep: 15 minutes Cook: 10 minutes —  Age: from 9 months

140g (5oz/generous 1 cup) self-raising flour (see page 61 to make your own), plus extra for dusting

30g (1oz/¼ cup) wholemeal flour (or more self-raising flour)

2 teaspoons extra virgin olive oil

140g (5oz/generous ½ cup) Greek yoghurt or dairy-free Greek-style yoghurt

40g (1½oz) pitted green olives, roughly chopped

60g (2oz/½ cup) grated Cheddar, Parmesan or dairy-free cheese

1. Preheat the oven to 200°C/180°C fan/400°F/ gas 6 and line a baking tray with baking paper.

2. Combine the flours, olive oil and yogurt in a bowl. Stir to bring together into a dough.

3. Tip out the dough onto a lightly floured surface and knead until it forms a smooth ball. Add more flour if needed to prevent sticking.

4. Knead in the chopped olives and grated cheese, ensuring they are evenly distributed throughout the dough.

5. Divide the dough into 16 portions. Roll each portion between your palms to form thin sticks, about 20cm (8 inches) long.

6. Arrange the breadsticks on the prepared baking tray, then bake in the oven for 10–12 minutes, or until lightly browned.

7. Remove from the oven and allow to cool slightly before serving. Buon appetito!

 **STORAGE** Store in an airtight container for 3 days, or freeze for up to 3 months. Defrost overnight in the fridge, or at room temperature for a few hours.

 **TIPS** To save time, you can also roll the dough into a large rectangle and cut into 10 thin breadsticks.

Though you might worry about the salt content of olives, including a small amount in your baby's diet, like that used here, is beneficial for their exposure to different tastes.

Cheese and Olive
Breadsticks

Homemade
Hummus

# SWEET POTATO CRACKERS

Grace and Kate love crackers, especially when served with hummus as a dip. While shop-bought ones are handy, I enjoy making their favourites at home. It's a great way to choose what ingredients to use, and the girls love helping me bake them. You can cut them into squares or use pastry cutters to create fun shapes.

    Makes: 50–60 crackers  Prep: 15 minutes Cook: 25 minutes  Age: from 6 months

170g (6oz) sweet potato, peeled and roughly chopped

50g (1¾oz/½ cup) finely grated Parmesan, Cheddar or dairy-free cheese, plus extra for sprinkling

40ml (1¼ fl oz) extra virgin olive oil or melted unsalted butter

120g (4¼oz/1 cup) wholemeal or plain flour

1. Preheat the oven to 180°C/160°C fan/350°F/gas 4.

2. Steam the sweet potato over a gentle heat for 15–20 minutes until soft, then set aside to cool. Once cooled, weigh out 140g (5oz) of the potato (any leftovers can be discarded or saved for later use).

3. Combine the mashed sweet potato, cheese and oil or butter in a large bowl and mix well.

4. Gradually incorporate the flour, using your hands to bring the mixture together into a ball of dough.

5. Tip out the dough onto a sheet of baking paper and roll it out until about 5mm (¼ inch) thick (remember, thinner dough yields crispier crackers).

6. Use a sharp knife or pizza cutter to slice the dough into your desired shapes.

7. Transfer the baking paper onto a baking sheet and use a fork to prick the crackers all over. Lightly sprinkle with a little more cheese.

8. Bake in the oven for 10–15 minutes, or until the edges turn lightly brown.

9. Remove from the oven and allow to cool completely before serving – they'll continue to firm up as they cool. Buon appetito!

**STORAGE** Store in an airtight container for 2–3 days.

# ENERGY BALLS

These are my favourite snacks for a quick, tasty energy boost. I originally made them for myself when the girls were little, but now the whole family, including Mattia, loves them! They're super easy to make and last for weeks in the fridge. So, you can make a bunch and enjoy them whenever you need a yummy treat.

   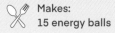 Makes: 15 energy balls  Prep: 10 minutes   Age: from 2 years

150g (5½oz/⅔ cup) smooth peanut butter

60g (2oz/¼ cup) maple syrup

100g (3½oz/1 cup) ground almonds

2 tablespoons milled seeds of your choice

30g (1oz) dark chocolate, chopped

1. Combine the peanut butter and maple syrup in a bowl and mix to combine.

2. Add the remaining ingredients and mix well until combined.

3. Scoop 2 teaspoons of the dough into your hand and roll it into a ball. Repeat until all the mixture has been used up.

4. Chill in the fridge for 20–30 minutes to set.

5. Buon appetito!

 **STORAGE**  Store in an airtight container in the fridge for up to 2 weeks.

**TIPS**  Want to make bars instead? Press the dough into a loaf pan before chilling, then cut into bars and enjoy!

# FOUR-INGREDIENT BREAKFAST BARS

This has been one of the most popular reels on my Instagram page, so it couldn't be missed here. Bananas are a rich source of vitamin C and are packed with prebiotic fibre – the preferred 'food' for good gut bacteria.

    Makes: 10 bars  Prep: 5 minutes Cook: 35 minutes  Age: from 6 months

**NOTE: don't add the chocolate for children under 2 years old**

240g (8½oz) overripe bananas

120g (4¼oz/1¼ cups) porridge oats

2 tablespoons smooth peanut butter (or any nut or seed butter)

1 big handful of dark chocolate chips (optional)

virgin coconut oil or unsalted butter, for greasing

1. Preheat the oven to 180°C/160°C fan/350°F/gas 4 and lightly grease a 20 x 20cm (8 x 8 inch) baking dish or line it with baking paper.

2. Mash the bananas in a bowl, then add the remaining ingredients and mix well.

3. Transfer to the prepared baking dish, then bake in the oven for 35–40 minutes, or until golden brown on top.

4. Remove from the oven and allow to cool completely before slicing into bars.

5. Buon appetito!

 **STORAGE** Store in an airtight container for up to 3 days, or freeze for up to 3 months. Defrost in the fridge overnight.

You can warm them up in a low oven before serving, if desired.

 **TIPS** You can swap the chocolate for chopped blueberries, strawberries or raspberries.

# YOGHURT POUCHES

When we go to the supermarket, my girls always ask me to buy yoghurt pouches or tubes – they love them! But while shop-bought varieties are convenient, they often contain excess sugar, added flavourings and preservatives. That's why I decided to make them at home with wholesome ingredients whenever possible. These homemade yoghurt pouches are easily customisable, healthier and convenient.

    Serves: 2 children  Prep: 5 minutes  Age: from 6 months

**NOTE: don't add the honey or maple syrup for babies under 1 year old**

100g (3½oz) strawberries or your fruit of choice

200g (7oz/¾ cup) Greek yoghurt or dairy-free Greek-style yoghurt

3 tablespoons maple syrup or honey, plus extra as needed (optional)

1. Put the fruit, half the yoghurt and the maple syrup or honey into a blender. Blend on medium-low until smooth.

2. Add the remaining yoghurt and stir by hand, adjusting the sweetness to taste.

3. Pour the yoghurt mixture into glasses or reusable pouches or tubes.

4. Buon appetito!

 **STORAGE** Store in in the fridge for up to 3 days. Shake or stir well before serving.

**TIPS** You can use your favourite fruits or mix several together to create different combinations. Our favourites are banana, blueberries, mango and peach.

# ITALIAN-STYLE HOT CHOCOLATE

Since moving to London, one of the things I miss most during the winter is Italian hot chocolate. It's rich and creamy, and an absolute delight with every spoonful! So, I tried recreating the recipe to share this goodness with my daughters, and now with all of you too.

    Serves: 2 children    Prep: 5 minutes Cook 10 minutes    Age: from 2 years

8g (¼oz) unsweetened cacao powder

15g (½oz) light brown soft sugar

10g (⅓oz) cornflour

250ml (8fl oz/1 cup) whole cow's milk or plant-based milk alternative

30g (1oz) dark chocolate, chopped

1. Combine the cacao powder, sugar and cornflour in a small saucepan. Add a little of the milk and whisk until smooth and lump-free.

2. Place the saucepan over a medium-high heat, then gradually pour in the remaining milk while stirring continuously and simmer for 5–8 minutes until thick and creamy.

3. Remove from the heat and add the chopped dark chocolate. Stir well until the chocolate is completely melted, then serve immediately.

4. Buon appetito!

 **TIPS**   If the hot chocolate becomes too thick, simply thin it out with a bit of milk.

If you desire a sweeter drink, you can add sugar to taste, even after cooking.

# PURPLE SMOOTHIE/ICE POP

I've found smoothies to be a lifesaver for busy mornings and snacks. Made only with ingredients you can store in your freezer or pantry, they're a quick and nutritious choice. Did you know that dark-skinned fruits and vegetables (like blueberries) are packed full of antioxidants?

     Serves: 2 children     Prep: 5 minutes     Age: from 6 months

**NOTE: don't add the honey for babies under 1 year old**

1 ripe banana

40g (1½oz/¼ cup) frozen blueberries

1 heaped tablespoon smooth peanut butter (or any nut or seed butter)

150ml (5fl oz/scant ⅔ cup) whole cow's milk or plant-based milk alternative

1 tablespoon raw manuka honey (optional)

1 teaspoon seeds of your choice, such as chia seeds, hemp seeds or flaxseeds

1. Combine all the ingredients in a blender and blend until smooth.

2. Serve immediately.

3. Buon appetito!

 **STORAGE** Enjoy fresh or pour into ice-lolly moulds to make healthy and delicious ice lollies, ready for the hottest days! Freeze for up to 3 months.

 **TIPS** If your little one is allergic to nuts, then switch the peanut butter with a seed butter (sunflower, pumpkin, etc.) or leave it out.

SNACKS

# BANANA PEANUT GELATO

This banana 'nice cream' is so easy and delicious! It's also a great way to use up old bananas as they can stay frozen for weeks, so you'll always be prepared for those sudden hot summer days craving ice cream!

    Serves: 4 children  Prep: 5 minutes  Age: from 6 months

4 large overripe bananas, peeled and thinly sliced

2 tablespoons smooth peanut butter

1. Arrange the banana slices in a single layer on a large plate or baking sheet and freeze for at least 2–3 hours.

2. Transfer the frozen banana slices to a food processor and blend for 1–2 minutes until smooth and creamy, scraping down the bowl as needed.

3. Add the peanut butter and blend to combine.

4. Serve immediately for a soft-serve ice cream consistency. If you prefer harder ice cream, scrape into an airtight container or individual containers and place in the freezer for a few hours before serving.

5. Buon appetito!

 **STORAGE** Freeze for up to 4 months. Let it sit at room temperature for 5–10 minutes to soften slightly before serving.

 **TIPS** If you have a hard time creating a creamy consistency, you can add 1–2 tablespoons milk to help blend the banana slices.

You can also freeze the mixture into ice-lolly moulds to make ice lollies.

# STRAWBERRY FROZEN YOGHURT

In the summer, there's nothing better than cooling off with some gelato! Grace and Kate absolutely love it, so I always try to offer them a healthier alternative using real ingredients. With just three ingredients and a blender, you can make this frozen yoghurt in 5 minutes!

    Serves: 6 children 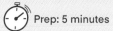 Prep: 5 minutes  Age: from 6 months

**NOTE: don't add the honey or maple syrup for babies under 1 year old**

200g (7oz/1½ cups) frozen strawberries

50g (1¾oz) Greek yoghurt or dairy-free Greek-style yoghurt

2–3 tablespoons honey or maple syrup (optional)

1. Put the frozen strawberries, yoghurt and honey, if using, into a food processor and blend for 3–4 minutes until smooth and thick, scraping down the bowl as needed.

2. Serve immediately for a soft-serve ice cream consistency. If you prefer harder ice cream, scrape into an airtight container or individual containers and place in the freezer for a few hours before serving.

3. Buon appetito!

 **STORAGE** Freeze for up to 4 months. Let it sit at room temperature for 5–10 minutes to soften slightly before serving.

 **TIPS** Be careful not to over-blend the mixture as it may become too soft.

Experiment with different frozen fruits to create your favourite flavour.

You can also freeze the mixture into ice-lolly moulds to make ice lollies.

SNACKS

# STRAWBERRY CHIA JAM

Quick, easy and thickened with chia instead of sugar, this jam is delicious and made with real ingredients, so perfect for feeding your little one. You can use fresh or frozen fruit, so it's also great for using up summer leftovers.

    Makes: 1 small jar  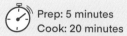 Prep: 5 minutes Cook: 20 minutes   Age: from 6 months

**NOTE: don't add the maple syrup for babies under 1 year old**

150g (5½oz/1 cup) frozen or fresh strawberries, hulled and chopped

1 tablespoon chia seeds

1 tablespoon maple syrup (optional)

1. Put the strawberries into a small saucepan over a low heat and cook for 5–10 minutes until soft.

2. Mash the softened strawberries with a fork or a potato masher until smooth.

3. Stir in the chia seeds and maple syrup, if using, then continue to cook for a further 15 minutes, stirring occasionally.

4. Remove from the heat and transfer to a bowl. The jam will thicken as it cools.

5. Buon appetito!

**STORAGE**  Store in an airtight container in the fridge for up to 1 week.

**TIPS**  Mix it up with different berries and try your favourite combos!

Use as a spread on toast, waffles or pancakes, or mix into yogurt or porridge for a delicious treat.

# SPECIAL OCCASIONS

# FIRST BIRTHDAY CAKE

I made this birthday cake for Kate's first birthday. It's perfect for celebrating this big day since it's sweetened only with fruit. Decorating it with the healthy icing adds extra excitement for your little one to dive into as well. I loved seeing Kate's enthusiasm when she smashed it!

   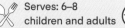 Serves: 6–8 children and adults  Prep: 20 minutes Cook: 25 minutes  Age: from 6 months

150g (5½oz) ripe bananas, mashed

110g (4oz) crisp eating apple, peeled, cored and finely grated

2 medium eggs or 60g (2oz/¼ cup) applesauce

120g (4¼oz) unsalted butter or dairy-free butter, melted

200g (7oz/1⅔ cups) wholemeal or plain flour

2 teaspoons baking powder

**FOR THE ICING**

150g (5½oz/⅔ cup) mascarpone or dairy-free cream cheese

100g (3½oz/⅓ cup) Greek yoghurt or dairy-free Greek-style yoghurt

2–3 tablespoons maple syrup (optional)

1. Preheat the oven to 180°C/160°C fan/350°F/gas 4. Grease two 15cm (6 inch) round cake tins and line the bottoms with baking paper.

2. Combine the bananas, apple, eggs or applesauce and melted butter in a large bowl.

3. In another bowl, sift together the flour and baking powder.

4. Gradually add the dry ingredients to the wet ingredients, mixing until just combined.

5. Divide the batter evenly between the prepared cake tins and smooth the tops. Bake in the oven for 25–30 minutes, or until a skewer inserted into the centre comes out clean.

6. Remove the cakes from the oven and allow to cool in the tins for 10 minutes before turning out onto a wire rack to cool completely.

7. Meanwhile, prepare the icing. Whisk together the mascarpone, yoghurt and maple syrup until smooth.

8. Place one cake on a platter or cake plate. Spread with half the icing, then place the second cake on top, pressing down gently. Spread the remaining icing on top.

9. Buon compleanno!

**STORAGE** Store in an airtight container in the fridge for up to 3 days, or wrap tightly and freeze for up to 2 months

Defrost in the fridge overnight.

**TIPS** To line the cake tins, trace around the tin onto baking paper and cut out two circles.

This cake is naturally sweetened with fruit. For added sweetness, add 3–4 tablespoons coconut or brown sugar.

You can decorate the cake with chopped soft fruits, such as strawberries or blueberries, for a colourful and nutritious finish.

# CHRISTMAS TREE CRACKERS

Christmas is my favourite time of year, and I love nothing more than surprising my little ones with themed treats. These Christmas tree-shaped crackers are perfect for adding a festive touch to snack time. Get your child involved by letting them help with cutting out the shapes. It's a fun activity that brings joy to the kitchen and creates lasting memories together.

    Makes: 40 crackers   Prep: 15 minutes Cook: 10 minutes   Age: from 6 months

20g (¾oz) basil leaves

40g (1½oz) unsalted butter or dairy-free butter, melted

180g (6¼oz/¾ cup) Greek yoghurt or dairy-free Greek-style yoghurt

250g (9oz/2 cups) self-raising flour (see page 61 to make your own), plus extra for dusting

30g (1oz/⅓ cup) grated Parmesan cheese or vegan Parmesan

1. Preheat the oven to 180°C/160°C fan/350°F/gas 4 and line a baking sheet with baking paper.

2. Put the basil leaves and melted butter into a blender and pulse until smooth.

3. Pour the butter mixture into a large bowl, then stir in the yoghurt and flour and use your hands to bring together into a dough.

4. Tip the dough out onto a lightly floured surface or sheet of baking paper and roll it out to 5mm (¼ inch) thick, then use a Christmas tree pastry cutter to cut out Christmas tree shapes.

5. Arrange the trees on the prepared baking sheet, then bake for 10–12 minutes until the edges just start to turn golden, keeping an eye on them to ensure they don't burn.

6. Remove from the oven and allow to cool before serving.

7. Buon appetito!

 **STORAGE** Store in an airtight container for up to 3 days, or freeze for up to 3 months. Defrost in the fridge overnight or at room temperature for a few hours.

SPECIAL OCCASIONS

# HALLOWEEN QUESADILLA

Kids love this recipe! The quesadillas only take a few minutes to prepare and with their Halloween twist, they bring a touch of spooky fun to your dinner table, making you the cool parent who serves up fun Halloween food! Plus, they are picky eater-friendly!

 VEGETARIAN

 Serves: 1 child

 Prep: 5 minutes
Cook: 5 minutes

 Age: from 6 months

1 small tortilla

1 large egg

20g (¾oz) carrot, peeled, grated and squeezed to remove excess water

20g (¾oz) Cheddar cheese, grated

extra virgin olive oil or unsalted butter, for cooking

1. Cut out a jack-o'-lantern face from the tortilla using a sharp knife. Get creative!

2. Combine the egg, carrot and cheese in a bowl and mix well.

3. Heat a little oil or butter in a small frying pan over a medium heat, then pour the egg mixture into the pan and spread it out evenly.

4. Place the tortilla on top and cook for about 2–3 minutes, or until the egg is cooked.

5. Flip the tortilla with a spatula, then cook for another minute.

6. Buon appetito!

 **STORAGE** Store in an airtight container in the fridge for up to 2 days, or freeze for up to 3 months. Reheat in a frying pan with a little butter or in a panini press to avoid it becoming soggy.

 **TIPS** Choose a pan the same size as the tortilla.

SPECIAL OCCASIONS

# EASTER BUNNY PANCAKES

This breakfast is a must on Easter morning at our house. I've been making it since Grace was born, and it's a tradition I'll continue. So simple and cute, I'm sure your kids will love it too!

   Makes: 2 bunnies   Prep: 5 minutes / Cook: 10 minutes   Age: from 6 months

**NOTE: don't add chocolate chips or raisins for children under 2 years old**

1 small ripe banana

30g (1oz) Greek yoghurt or dairy-free Greek-style yoghurt

1 medium egg

40g (1½oz/⅓ cup) plain or wholemeal flour

⅓ teaspoon baking powder

virgin coconut oil or unsalted butter, for frying

**TO DECORATE**

Greek yoghurt or dairy-free Greek-style yoghurt

sliced bananas

1 handful of raisins or chocolate chips (optional)

1. Mash the banana in a bowl, then add the yoghurt, egg, flour and baking powder and mix until well combined.

2. Heat a little oil or butter in a frying pan over medium heat, then spoon in a generous dollop of batter in a round shape to create the bunny body. Add a smaller round for the head, two small ovals for feet, and two long, thin strips for ears.

3. Cook for 2–3 minutes, or until bubbles start to form on the top and the edges are set. Flip and cook for another minute until golden brown.

4. Arrange the bunny body in the middle of the plate. Position the head, ears and feet just overlapping to look like the back of a bunny. Add a small dollop of Greek yoghurt for the tail, a slice of banana on each foot and place three chopped raisins or chocolate chips, if using, under each banana to create the bunny's foot pads.

5. Buona Pasqua!

**STORAGE** Store in an airtight container in the fridge for up to 3 days. Freeze the pancakes individually on a baking sheet, then transfer to a freezer bag for up to 3 months. Reheat in a dry frying pan or in the microwave until warmed through.

# INDEX

# SPECIAL THANKS

## My husband and best friend

I would like to start by thanking the most important person to me, my best friend and husband, Mattia. Thank you for believing in me right from the start, perhaps even more than I believed in myself. I can never thank you enough for everything you do for me every single day, for supporting me and for your continuous encouragement to grow my career. Even though we are like cat and dog when we work together, I wouldn't want anyone else by my side but you, with your tenacity and dedication. Perhaps I don't say it enough, but thank you truly for everything, I love you.

## My daughters

A huge thank you to my wonderful little girls, Grace and Kate, who have been my muses and my trusted taste-testers. It is only because of you that Yummy Little Belly was born.

## My friends

I wish to express my deep gratitude to my friends Marika, Carla and Stephanie. Living in a country without one's own family, as you well know, is difficult. Your support, valuable advice and invaluable help during this journey have meant so much to me. Thank you from the bottom of my heart, my dear friends.

## My mother-in-law

Thank you, Laura, for being a wonderful grandmother to Grace and Kate, and thank you for coming to London to support me when I most needed it.

Looking after the girls while I was writing and testing recipes was a huge help, and it would have been impossible without you.

## My followers

I want to express my deepest gratitude to my followers, because it's thanks to each of you that I am where I am today. Your constant support and encouragement have been the driving force behind my journey. Every like, comment and share fills my heart with immense joy, but what motivates me most is receiving messages saying that I've made your life a little bit easier; this keeps me pushing forward. Thank you for trusting me and allowing me to come into your kitchen with my recipes. You have believed in me, inspired me and supported me through the toughest times. I am eternally grateful for the incredible community we have built together. Thank you, from the depth of my heart, for being part of this beautiful journey with me. Your presence means more than words can express. With all my love and gratitude, this book is dedicated to you. Thank you.

## Sophie Hinchliffe (Mrs Hinch)

This is a particular thank you I really wanted to include in this book.

With profound gratitude, thank you, Sophie! You were truly the springboard for my page! Without probably realising it, your tag not only gave the first exposure to Yummy Little Belly when it was just a little page on Instagram but also gave me the inspiration I needed at that time. Looking at you and what you created with your page truly inspired me to make Yummy Little Belly not just a hobby but my job! Thank you.

## Eco Rascals

Celeidh and Kristina, I remember the day we first exchanged a DM on Instagram like it was yesterday. You were the first company that believed in me. The day I received all your wonderful bamboos plates I was over the moon and I couldn't believe that someone was gifting these to me. I'm proud that three years later, the way we support each other hasn't changed.

## Agent

Thank you, Sarah, for your efforts and support during our collaboration. Your kindness and willingness to assist are greatly appreciated.

## Stylist

A heartfelt thank you to Roberta Rocca from @thestudioby, who selected all my outfits for this book. Roberta, your amazing work as the wardrobe stylist for my book has been invaluable, and along the way, you've also become a dear friend. Your support, creativity and friendship mean a lot to me.

## Publisher

4 October 2023 at 20:37

This is the day I received your email, Lydia, stating that HarperCollins was interested in publishing a Yummy Little Belly book. What a day! That night, I couldn't sleep as I started to imagine the book. Thank you, Lydia, for trusting me and bringing my first book to life.

## Paediatric dietitian

Lucy Upton, I truly appreciate your support and expertise in helping me with my book. Your guidance has made a significant difference, and I'm incredibly grateful for your contributions.

## Photographer and food stylist

Andrew and Rosie, I suppose I should start with an apology before expressing my gratitude. I'm sorry for all the last-minute changes during each day of the shoot! However, a huge thank you is in order for involving me in every single shot and making me feel comfortable enough to share my opinions. Thank you again for your incredible skills in capturing exactly what I was dreaming of for this book.

## HarperCollins and the team behind the book

Thank you to Catherine, Georgina and every single individual in this beautiful company who has made this possible. It's astonishing and unimaginable how many people are involved in publishing each book. So, thank you for your great work and support!

## Brands

A special thank you to the wonderful small businesses who so kindly gifted props to us for the photoshoot, and who I continue to work with: Eco Rascals, Scandiborn, KAOS, Liewood, Doddl and Trixie.